teatime *in* mogadishu

Ahmed's discussion of traditional Somali/Islamic peacemaking and restorative justice methods raises thought-provoking questions on gospel and culture. Ahmed's passion for peace with and within Islam is of huge importance for Christian-Muslim relations.
—*Dr. John Azumah, Director, Centre for Islamic Studies, London (UK) School of Theology*

An inspiring testimony to the tremendous impact of growing up in a loving family of faith, and of Ahmed's choice to live a Christ-centered life. Ahmed is a model of peacemaking in a pluralistic religious context.
—*Arli Klassen, Executive Director, Mennonite Central Committee, Akron, Pa.*

This book, shared in congregational small groups and classes, will help participants understand how Jesus became the way of peace for a Muslim youth. It will also invite others to invite Jesus to guide their life decisions and to step forward with their own peacemaking initiatives.
—*Elizabeth G. Nissley, Pastor, James Street Mennonite Church, Lancaster, Pa.*

Devotionally inspiring, missiologically instructive, and spiritually challenging. At a time when "Somali" and "Christian" seem like oxymorons in our religious vocabularies, this book is a heartening reminder that with God all things are possible.
—*Jonathan J. Bonk, Executive Director, Overseas Ministries Study Center, New Haven, Conn.*

Ahmed Ali Haile's deep appreciation for his Muslim heritage motivated him to continue serving his people at great personal sacrifice. Faith in Jesus Christ was the reservoir of the compassion, hospitality, and witness that characterized Ahmed over four decades. His legacy will inspire and challenge.
—*Wilbert R. Shenk, Fuller Graduate School of Intercultural Studies, Pasadena, Calif.*

A unique and powerful contribution to the great Somali tradition of storytelling. Simultaneously, it adds a compelling chapter to the contemporary Jesus story that will cheer and challenge the hearts and minds of people everywhere who long for peace and good news in a battered, desperate world.
—*Richard Showalter, President, Eastern Mennonite Missions, Salunga, Pa.*

Ahmed Ali Haile understands the strengths of Islam and pre-Islamic traditions in his development as a Somali and as a global peacemaker. He is also very clear that Christ-centered peace activism is what brings true transformation to individuals and to the social, economic, and even political structures they create.
—*Barry Hart, Director, Center for Justice and Peacebuilding, Eastern Mennonite University, Harrisonburg, Va.*

teatime *in* mogadishu

My Journey as a
Peace Ambassador
in the World of Islam

Ahmed Ali Haile
as told to David W. Shenk

The Christians Meeting Muslims series from Herald Press addresses central themes in Christian-Muslim engagement: dialogue, witness and invitation, and peacemaking. The titles in the series include *A Muslim and A Christian in Dialogue* by Badru D. Katerrega and David W. Shenk; *Journeys of the Muslim Nation and the Christian Church: Exploring the Mission of Two Communities* by David W. Shenk; and *Teatime in Mogadishu: My Journey as a Peace Ambassador in the World of Islam* by Ahmed Ali Haile.

Herald Press
Harrisonburg, Virginia
Waterloo, Ontario

Library of Congress Cataloging-in-Publication Data

Haile, Ahmed Ali.
 Teatime in Mogadishu : my journey as a peace ambassador in the world
of Islam / Ahmed Ali Haile as told to David W. Shenk.
  p. cm.
 ISBN 978-0-8361-9557-6 (pbk. : alk. paper)
  1. Haile, Ahmed Ali. 2. Christian converts from Islam—Somalia—Biography. 3. Christian converts from Islam—United States—Biography.
 4. Peace-building—Somalia. 5. Peace-building—Religious aspects—Mennonites. I. Shenk, David W., 1937- II. Title.
 BV2626.4.H35A3 2011
 248.2'46092—dc22
 [B]
                                      2011004734

Scripture quotations taken from the Holy Bible, New International Ver-
sion ® Copyright © 1973, 1978, 1984 by the International Bible Society.
Used by permission of Zondervan Publishing House. All rights reserved.

Qu'ran quotations are from The Holy Qur'an, Text, Translation, and
Commentary, by Abdullah Yusuf Ali. Published (1987) by Tahrike Tarsile
Qur'an.

Copyright © 2011 by Herald Press, Harrisonburg, VA 22802
 Released simultaneously in Canada by Herald Press,
 Waterloo, Ont. N2L 6H7. All rights reserved
Library of Congress Control Number: 2011004734
International Standard Book Number: 978-0-8361-9557-6
Printed in the United States of America
Cover by Reuben Graham
Interior design by Gwen M. Stamm

16 15 14 13 12 11 10 9 8 7 6 5 4 3 2

To order or request information please call 1-800-245-7894 or visit
www.heraldpress.com.

Dedicated to

My wife—Martha Jean Wilson

who has been my faithful and loving companion, encouraging me in the way of Christ and serving as counselor and partner in ministry while also being a loving mother.

Our children—Afrahyare, Sofia, Gedi

who bless me with joy, who have deep roots in East Africa and North America, and who have invested generously in my commitments to peacemaking.

My parents—Ali Haile Afrah and Hersia Shirar

who nurtured me and loved me and who planted in my soul a yearning to know and serve God faithfully.

Ahmed is a synonym for Muhammad. My parents named me Ahmed in respect for the prophet of Islam. Ahmed also means a person who is worthy of honor. Nearly five decades ago God honored me by calling me to be an emissary of the peace of Christ within the world of Islam, with a special commitment to the Somali Muslim people.

Contents

Foreword

*How beautiful on the mountains are the feet of those
who bring good news, who proclaim peace, who bring
good tidings, who proclaim salvation....*
—Isaiah

As I write, before me is today's *New York Times* reporting that
the Shabab insurgence killed at least thirty in a hotel in Somalia's capital, Mogadishu, yesterday, a day after shelling government positions and killing dozens of people. This spirit of violence is akin to the spirit of those who tried to kill Ahmed Ali
Haile, the author of this memoir, over eighteen years ago, as he
was seeking to reconcile fighting clans. Colleagues amputated
much of his injured leg with knives to save his life. When necrotizing fasciitis started its destructive process in his leg, those
who risked their lives to get him medevacked to Nairobi were
the clan leaders he was seeking to reconcile.

The events that led him there started in his youth as he was
raised by his upright Muslim parents; however, he chose to follow Jesus and thereby followed in the footsteps of the first
recorded Muslim convert to Christianity, who was part of a migra-
tion of some of Muhammad's early companions to Abyssinia.
This region is referred to by Arab historians as Habash or
Habasha, a designation that sometimes included not only the
present land of Ethiopia but also the Horn of Africa, hence at
least part if not all of present-day Somalia. Yet, unlike the first
Muslim convert to Christ, who is generally understood to have
gone to East Africa to avoid conflict in seventh-century Mecca,
the contemporary convert Ahmed returned to the region repeat-
edly to mediate conflict.

Ahmed's pilgrimage has many lessons to offer in the current

religious, ethnic, and clan turmoil. First, his Muslim upbringing prepared him to see its fulfillment in the gospel. He found in Islam and the local pre-Islamic cultural influence, redemptive analogies or prototypes of redemption through Christ; therefore, he never criticized his former faith.

Secondly, he utilized peacemaking tools of the courts and laws inherited from the colonial period, the qadi courts and laws of Islamic Sharia, the pre-Islamic systems of justice in covenantal relations and responsibilities, plus input from psychology and sociology. But he found that ultimately it was the gospel that could end the cycle of retaliation as it was absorbed by Christ and his cross and the Holy Spirit who through the church reconciled people to God and each other.

Yet this story is not just a listing of peacemaking theories and lessons. Rather, they emerge from the interaction of a flesh and blood person with concrete events. His commitments to transformative peacemaking were expressed amidst enormous countervailing challenges. In time his advocates and protectors included an imam who at one time had called for his execution for apostasy.

I met Ahmed, minus a leg, a few years ago. As I reflect on Isaiah's words, "How beautiful on the mountains are the feet of those...who proclaim peace...who proclaim salvation" (Isaiah 52:7), his foot is truly beautiful. As you read his story, you cannot but say the same.

—*J. Dudley Woodberry*
Dean Emeritus and Senior Professor of Islamic Studies
School of Intercultural Studies
Fuller Theological Seminary, Pasadena, Calif.

Preface

AHMED Ali Haile hails from Bulo Burte in central Somalia. He was Muslim and until he was fifteen all his friends and acquaintances were Muslims. In his mid-teens Christ met him. In response to God's call, Ahmed has become an enthusiastic captive of Christ. His ministry has been international, but his first commitment is to the Somali Muslim people among whom he has been an ambassador of the gospel of peace. His journey has been filled with unimaginable challenge. Yet in it all, Ahmed has served his people with abandonment.

When I first met him, Ahmed was chuckling, a rippling joyous chuckle, sharing a joke with friends. We met at a festival in the heart of metropolitan Mogadishu, the capital city of the Somali Democratic Republic. That was October 21, 1972, when the Somali nation was celebrating the third anniversary of its Marxist-Leninist revolution. That revolution had violently swept away the Somali clan-based parliamentary democracy that had governed since independence in 1960.

However, when I met Ahmed his first loyalties were not to the Marxist revolution. He was, in fact, committed to a radically different revolution. The year before our meeting this tall eighteen-year-old youth had sealed in baptism his commitment to the life-giving revolution of Christ. He was baptized in the offshore waters of the Indian Ocean. We did not imagine on that festive day in Mogadishu that our paths would often cross, and that our lives would knit together in the bonds of faith nurtured in mutual commitment to Christ and the church.

Neither did we imagine the astonishing four-decade adventure that the journey with Christ would bring into Ahmed's life. As a disciple of Jesus, he has zestfully engaged both the secularist technological world of the West and the fluid and sometimes tumultuous dynamism of Somali and Islamic cultures within the grand mix of Marxist ideology and clan-based politics. His has been an incredible adventure touched with pathos and tragedy as well as quiet accomplishments and impossible victories.

Nearly four decades after our first conversation, my wife, Grace, and I had a very different meeting with Ahmed and his wife, Martha. They were visiting our mutual friends, Kenneth and Elizabeth Nissley, in their home in Lancaster, Pennsylvania, in the United States. It was August 2009. Ahmed was struggling with cancer, and he and his family had just returned from East Africa for reprieve and medical care. It was there that Ahmed Haile shared a compelling conviction.

Although weakened by chemotherapy and his illness, Ahmed spoke forcefully, "I do not know how long I will live, but I do know that my story should be written for both Muslims and Christians. It is a story that includes a deep appreciation for my Muslim background and my family. It is a story that bears witness that when I met Jesus and the church, I came home. My Muslim heritage prepared me to believe in Jesus Christ. I want you, David, to work with me in writing my story. That is my request to you, my dear friend. Martha will help."

Then he said simply, "I am tired. Let's pray and then I need to rest."

After prayer we embraced as we said our farewells. He stood on his one leg supported by his crutches. Ahmed has lived with one leg for many years, because his right leg was shattered in a rocket attack when he was attempting to forge a peace agreement among clan factions in Somalia. I have sometimes joked with Ahmed that he is my dear friend, the one-legged peacemaker. More seriously, Ahmed has persisted in peacemaking even after that attack, which not only severed his leg but nearly took his life. That persistence has earned him enormous credibility within Muslim communities committed to peacemaking, especially in East Africa. This obvious mark of suffering for peace has also positioned him for serious engagement with the militant fringes of jihadist movements.

Grace and I knew our response to Ahmed's request had to be, "Yes!"

Three months later Grace and I were in the Midwest not far from where the Hailes live in Glendale just north of Milwaukee, Wisconsin. We met in the home of Dr. Marc and Nancy Erickson who had been friends of the Hailes for many years. For five days we were immersed in Ahmed's story. Sometimes we shared in tears, other times joyous laughter at the amazement of it all. We recorded the interview. Alas, the first couple of hours were hopelessly garbled when early on, in a burst of exhilarating response to what Ahmed was saying, I jumped from my chair, dropping the recording device into my glass of hot apple cider. Not to be deflected, we bought a new recorder and continued the marathon listening. Martha was at hand to add her insight and contribute her story as well.

The interview developed within a persistent health challenge for Ahmed. His health was precarious and he was on exhausting therapies. We jostled the times of interviews to make space for the therapies he was undergoing. Our pattern was to listen to a segment of his story, and then he would say, "Now I am tired." So he would retire for rest until he was ready to continue with the recording process.

As we were about to leave for our next appointment, we stood in a circle for prayer. Ahmed reminded us, "Do not forget that when I met Jesus, I knew I had come home. So whether I live or die doesn't really matter, for my calling now and in eternity is to glorify Jesus Christ. That is what this memoir is about."

A couple of weeks later Grace began tediously transcribing some thirty hours of interviews. We were unable to connect our recording device to a transcriber, so she worked the on and off mechanism manually. The dexterity of her hands amazed me. Then in January, a couple months later, I returned to Glendale for another day of interviews going over the 200 pages of transcribed material and filling in the gaps. Ahmed expanded certain themes: for example, traditional approaches to peacemaking in comparison to Christ-centered peacemaking. That was a good day, much of it just the two of us conversing together, with Martha slipping in occasionally. They are blessed with three children. Afrah was away in college, but Gedi and Sofia were in and out adding their humor and wit to the enterprise.

After I had completed the draft of the manuscript, we met for a third round of discussions, the four of us: Ahmed, Martha, Grace, and me. Prior to our meeting we participated in a fellowship time for friends of the Hailes at Landis Homes near Lancaster, Pennsylvania. This is a retirement community where a number of the former missionaries to Somalia now reside. Ahmed requested this gathering as a time for farewell. It was an extraordinary meeting; we reminisced and of course sang our favorite Somali gospel songs!

Then we met in the home of Kenneth and Elizabeth Nissley to review the manuscript. Although Ahmed was weary from the meetings with friends, he persisted with resilient focus, meticulously reviewing the manuscript. Martha would read aloud, while we all followed with written texts before us. She read until Ahmed would raise his right index finger and say, "Stop!" He would then elaborate on how he wanted it to be said. Sometimes he would say, "That paragraph adds nothing important—omit it." Late Sunday evening we were nearly finished, when Kenneth and Elizabeth appeared with a snack and a Bible for a wrap-up time of fellowship and prayer. Very early the next morning, Ahmed and Martha were leaving for Milwaukee. It was time to retire.

Several months later in July, the Haile family returned to Lancaster for a Somali and missionary reunion. James Street Mennonite Church hosted the 150 who came from across North America and one even coming from the United Kingdom. It was a joyous gathering for fellowship, feasting on a Somali traditional meal of goat and rice, and giving thanks for the providence of God in creating deep friendship between mostly Muslim Somalis and the missionaries.

After that gathering we met again in the Nissley home with the Hailes for final details. Two of the Haile children, Sofia and Gedi, were upstairs. I called them down and urged these well-poised teenagers, "Tell us one important reality about your father that must be included in this book."

They squirmed; there was an awkward silence.

Then Ahmed spoke with a quizzical chuckle, "I know why

you won't say anything. It is because you want to say, 'Our father is a dictator.' But you are too kind to say that!"

"Oh, no!" they exclaimed. "You are not a dictator."

Then they turned to me and for the next half hour talked energetically about hospitality. "Our father is characterized by hospitality. He welcomed everyone who came to our home. Hospitality is welcoming the guest even when it is not convenient. For our father the guest was never an inconvenience, even when the guest would come unannounced very late at night."

I interjected, "I suppose that hospitality meant that you had to give up your bed sometimes."

"Of course!" they emphasized. "But the many guests who stayed in our home had the opportunity to see a Christian family interacting in love and respect for one another. Father's hospitality, in which we all participated, was an expression of the love of Christ for the many refugees whom we cared for."

It is not only refugees who have experienced Ahmed's hospitality. Quite often, Grace and I have also experienced the hospitality of this home with entrées of chicken or goat and with exuberant conversation. Even when inconvenient, we have been welcomed!

I have written or edited well over a dozen books but this one has captivated me as none other. I am writing with a dear friend, but more importantly, I have been tremendously changed as I have been immersed in Ahmed's journey with Christ amidst daunting challenges and obstacles, most of it within the world of Islam. I have been touched deeply as I have listened to Ahmed interweave his dramatic autobiographical narrative with astute theological and missional reflection on themes that are exceedingly pertinent today.

This memoir is an invitation to listen. What difference does Jesus make for Ahmed whose heritage has been authentic Islam? What difference does Jesus make for Ahmed whose family has been respected as upright and genuinely religious? What is the treasure that Ahmed found in Christ and the church that compelled him to the conviction that in Jesus Christ, "I have come home"? How did Ahmed preserve and fulfill his calling to be an ambassador of the peace of Christ within the world of Islam?

At the end of this book, there is a study guide for groups interested in exploring together the implications of Ahmed's journey.

—*David W. Shenk*
Global Consultant
Eastern Mennonite Missions, Salunga, Pa.

CHAPTER 1

Muslim-Somali Heritage
Bulo Burte
(1953–68)

Say: He is God the One and Only;
God, the Eternal, Absolute.
—Qur'an

I AM Ahmed Ali Haile, the son of Ali Haile Afrahyare and Hersia Shirar. My hometown is Bulo Burte in central Somalia. Bulo Burte, or Dusty Village, is a wind-swept enclave nestled against the Shebelli River, whose tributaries retrieve life-giving rainfall from the Ethiopian highlands far to the western horizon. The short rainy seasons can be fickle and sparse and the dry seasons long and dusty. Bulo Burte is the principal hub for the wide-ranging camel herding nomads who traverse a thousand miles a year in their grand circular trek in the scrublands of the vast eastern Horn of Africa, questing for water and acacia shrub. However, my family was not nomadic; we preferred the more sedentary ways of Somali town life.

My parents: Somali mavericks
My parents were Somali mavericks. My mother was fourteen or fifteen years old when she married my father; she was my father's first wife, an exquisitely beautiful Somali maiden. However, their marriage was unusual for it was outside of the expectations of our clans. My mother and father came from two sub-clans that did not intermarry because the aura of my mother's

clan was deemed to be more powerful than my father's clan. The sages of our clans believed that for pregnancy to happen there needed to be the right mixture of complementary power. Alas, since the power of my mother's clan overwhelmed that of my father's clan, her marriage would immunize her against bearing children to my father. So the clan elders advised my father to divorce my mother and find a new wife whose power complemented rather than overwhelmed his power.

My father loved his young wife, Hersia. So rather than divorce her, my father invited the elders of Hersia's clan and his father-in-law to gather and bless his head with empowerment. At that time the elders also blessed my mother, declaring that she would bear eight sons. So my birth in 1953 in Bulo Burte, in central Somalia, was a special blessing, as were the births of my siblings. In fact, my mother bore nine sons, but one of them was a miscarriage.

Later my father married other wives as well. They bore him two additional sons and seven girls—seventeen children in all. The sons born to my mother were Mohammed, Mahmud, Abdullahi, Ahmed (myself), Hussein, Yassin, and then twins, Hassan and Othman. I was in the middle with four younger brothers. I became the leader and caretaker of my four younger siblings. It is amazing how scattered we have become: three of my brothers now live in the United States, two in Canada, three in Bulo Burte, and one in Mogadishu, Somalia.

Before his marriage in 1936, my father worked for the Italian military in their corps of engineers. After the defeat of the fascist Italian regime in World War II, my father was employed as a prison warden with the British military. He was placed in Mogadishu, in Johar, and then back in Mogadishu. Finally he was assigned to Bulo Burte where he was given an honorable discharge at about the time when British authority over southern Somalia ended and the European post-war peace agreements took effect.

These jobs introduced my father to a world beyond the horizons of Somali ethnocentrism. As a military officer, he earned the reputation of being a kind and fair man. When he left the military he developed a variety of businesses based in Bulo

Burte: grain fields irrigated from the Shebelli River or depend-
ent on rain, nomadic animal husbandry (cattle, camels, and
goats), vegetable gardening, a general grocery store, and im-
porting bananas from Merca, 160 miles (260 kilometers) to the
south. Father worked hard and whatever he touched prospered.

The dusty village

Although Dusty Village might not be an auspicious name, we
loved Bulo Burte. The wind-blown dust of the dry season not
withstanding, this town was a delightful community. I consider
the Bulo Burte of my childhood as a town with abundant social
capital.[1] That is to say, we were a healthy society and my family represented the best of that health. The prophet Jeremiah
describes the Rechabites, who embraced their father's upright
values (Jer 35:1-19); so also we children of Ali Haile Afrah cherished his wisdom. It is important for all societies to nurture their
social capital; we nurtured our father's social capital and determined not to deviate from his righteous example.

The tragedy of much of Somalia in the last two decades is
that precious social capital has been squandered. Fifty years
ago, my father worried about that. He fretted that his sons or
daughters might become lazy and cease living life generously.
He knew that laziness and selfishness erodes the qualities needed for a healthy society.

One of his proverbs stays in my soul:

> Soor a la sheegay saara kac,
> Soof a la sheegay sin u dhac.

The food is ready.
    It is time to eat.
    I will get up!
It is time to work.
    Now I will lay down.
    I can't go to work.
    I am sick.

His point was that people always arise from their rest when the
food is ready; in contrast, too often we continue with our rest

when there is work at hand. We need to arise for work just as enthusiastically as we arise when there is food.

A rich heritage

Both my father and mother came from respected family genealogies going back some fifteen generations. They were upright and generous. Mother never put water in the milk that she sold, so she was trusted by all. At mealtime she often invited the destitute from the byways around our home, from whatever clan, to join us for the evening meal.

The diversity of my father's business enterprises ensured that our family always had plenty; even in famine we never went hungry. The integrity of his business dealings and township relations was such that he was respected by all. He paid no attention to clan, treating everyone equally. (That is one reason I will never mention the name of my clan in this memoir.) Father treated his workers fairly. He was considered a wise man, and his words did not go unheeded.

When I visited Bulo Burte some years ago shortly after my father's death, some of his workers came to me to confess that they had cheated Father. I responded, "I know my father would have forgiven you and so do I."

If a person was hungry, Father always gave generously, even beyond the required Islamic alms for the poor (*zakat*). On one occasion a relative came by who was in severe financial straits. Father gave him cash and a bull to take and sell for the additional money he needed.

One of my sisters protested, "Father, this bull is part of our livelihood and not to be given away."

My father's exuberant generosity surprised me. He asserted, "All that I have belongs to my children. You will have plenty even after the bull is sold."

Years later I read in Luke's Gospel about a father whose older son begrudged a calf for a festival welcoming his younger prodigal brother home (Luke 15:11-32). My father demonstrated the compassion of the father in that Gospel account!

I live gratefully within the shadow of the enduring values my parents modeled.

Childhood formation

I was a rambunctious child. When I was about five, I was loitering with friends in the shade of a tree where a donkey was tethered. Two of us climbed the tree and jumped on the donkey's back. Of course he bolted in a terrible fright. I was hurled from the back of the donkey and fell on my right arm. Ever since that terrific fall I have suffered nerve damage in my right arm. My mother saw the hand of God in this, as she did in all the events of life. She confided that she always hoped at least one of her sons would devote his life to leading people in the ways of God. This injury was confirmation in her spirit that I should not pursue business or farming as a life vocation, but rather focus on learning and teaching the Qur'an.

That would be a different road than the one chosen by the more warrior-like men of my father's clan. They were practical men, and commitment to belligerent conflict, when necessary, was quite in line with their worldview. My grandfather, Afrahyare, was a recognized leader who was more impressed with the practical dimensions of survival than with time-consuming religious practices.

My more pious mother, on the other hand, cherished the more pacific lore of her people and communicated these values through her many proverbs and parables. One story she told, for example, was about a hungry beggar in rags:

> Once, while the beggar rested under an acacia tree, a bird perched above him chirping, "Prosperity is not good for a man, prosperity is not good for a man, prosperity is not good for a man!"
>
> Thereafter the beggar had the good fortune to be employed by a rich widow. Before long they married. But she warned her new husband, "Never look in the box under the bed. The day you look in that box our marriage will end."
>
> She and her husband prospered in their business enterprises. Yet he was not satisfied. He began to pester his wife, "I must also look inside the box under the bed. Why do you keep that secret from me?"
>
> Because of his pestering she finally agreed. She called all

the town elders and informed them of the agreement she
and her husband had made before they were married,
"The day my husband looks inside the secret box under
the bed, our marriage will end."

With excited anticipation her husband, the former beggar, opened the box in the presence of all the town elders.
He was appalled to find that the contents of the box were
his old, tattered and soiled beggar's clothing. So his wife
divorced him and sent him off with only his beggar's
clothes.

Truly the bird in the acacia tree got it right, "Prosperity
is not good for a man!"

The moral was that the avarice of demanding everything will
leave one in poverty. Such spiritual sensitivities of my mother's
have formed me deeply!

In 1965, when I was twelve, the rains failed. The Shebelli
River, with tributaries in the Ethiopian Highlands, dried up.
Our family migrated ninety miles south to Johar, where there
was still some fleeting greenery for our starving livestock. Soon
after, Mother had to return to Bulo Burte and I became respon-
sible for the four younger siblings. As a twelve-year-old I
learned to cook, organize, and lead. That event formed my leadership skills and taught me responsibility. When the rains
returned, we also returned to Bulo Burte, but by then most of
our livestock was gone.

Islam, my faith

Except for several obvious foreigners, all inhabitants of Bulo
Burte were Muslims. In fact, with very rare exceptions, all
Somalis were Muslims—including my parents. Most Somalis
traced their genealogy to their prophet Muhammad. They
believed that the blood of Muhammad and the faith of Islam
flowed in their veins. This meant that to be a Somali was to be
Muslim. So my identity was not only Somali, but also Muslim.

My mother's influence nudged me into beginning the journey
to Muslim spiritual leadership for which she felt I was destined.
At four years of age I was able to touch my left ear with my

right arm over my head; that meant I was mature enough to enroll in the *duksi* (Qur'anic school). I began memorizing the Qur'an in Arabic at the duksi. I approached this awesome commitment of receiving the powerful Qur'an into my being with appropriate sobriety. Although I struggled with the discipline of memorization more than some, I soon emerged as a leader among the students and became the teacher's assistant. By the time I was twelve I sometimes led in the *salat* (ritual prayers) that the faithful performed five times daily. Our mosque was Sunni Islam, as were all the inhabitants of Bulo Burte. As a child I became my mother's teacher, helping her learn some of the melodious cadences of the Arabic Qur'an. And I impressed upon her the central conviction of Islam: God is one.

As a devout Muslim, my mother received my teaching of the Qur'an with sober diligence. In fact, she developed the habit of reciting the *Al Ikhlas*[2] from the Qur'an 400 times every evening before retiring:

> In the name of Allah, Most Gracious, Most Merciful.
> Say: He is Allah the One and Only;
> Allah, the Eternal, Absolute;
> He begets not, nor is he begotten;
> And there is none like unto him.

Muslim authorities teach that this *surah* (chapter or section) is so central to the message of Islam that one recitation is equivalent to reading half the Qur'an.

I enjoyed studying Islam in the school within the mosque. There are four systems of Sharia (Islamic law) practiced by Sunni Muslims: Maliki, Hanbali, Hanafi, and Shafii. Somali Muslims follow the Shafii law that I studied after completing the memorization of the Qur'an and the rituals of prayer. The imam explained that there is a balance scale: submission to Islam is credited to the good side of the scale, and the wrongs that we do are placed on the debit side of the scale. At the final judgment, the shape of our scale will influence God's determination as to whether we will go to paradise or hell. So I quite enthusiastically did my salats and tried to obey Islamic law, hoping to add to the credit side of my scale.

The house of Islam

The Muslim community was referred to as the *ummah*, meaning "mother." The community has a mothering function, preserving, protecting, and nurturing the believer. The ummah is also referred to as the "house of Islam." I learned that this house is supported by ten pillars, five pillars of belief and five of duty.

The five pillars of belief are 1) belief in God; 2) belief in the prophets; 3) belief in the books of revelation; 4) belief in angels; 5) belief in the final judgment.

The imam taught us that the five pillars of duty are 1) the confession that there is no God but Allah, and Muhammad is the prophet of God (*shahadah*); 2) prayers five times daily facing Mecca (*salat*); 3) giving alms to the poor (*zakat*); 4) daytime fasting in the month of Ramadan (*sawm*); 5) going on the pilgrimage to Mecca once in a lifetime if possible (*hajj*).

As a faithful Muslim believer, I enjoyed living within the security of the house of Islam. I believed in the five supporting pillars of belief and I faithfully practiced the five pillars of duty. I enjoyed and felt secure within the Muslim ummah. That was my community. Sheikh Rashid was the imam. He was very effective in nurturing within my young soul an appreciation for Islam and the Muslim community.

One special memory of my immersion into the life of the mosque was the evenings when we Muslim disciples would sit in a circle with the imam, as he would expound on narratives that are referred to in the Qur'an. That was a challenging exercise, because the Qur'an does not present narratives in a cohesive way. Bits of narrative are alluded to here and there in the Qur'an as well as in the Hadith (Muslim traditions). I was amazed at the way Imam Sheikh Rashid could weave these fragments into a cohesive story. I was especially intrigued by the story of Joseph.

Some years later I was astonished to discover that the Bible more fully describes many of these sketchy allusions than does the Qur'an. That discovery was significant in my teenage years when I began to develop interest in the biblical narratives. The seed of that interest was sown in my soul in those evening storytelling circles with the imam.

Although I was secure within the house of Islam, my study of the Qur'an did not answer several perplexing questions within my young mind. However, I never felt free to ask any of the imams these questions. Most perplexing to me was the insistence that Muslims must believe all the books of God. The Qur'an specifically mentions the Scrolls of Abraham, the Torah of Moses, the Psalms of David, the Gospel of Jesus the Messiah, and, of course, the Qur'an. We Muslims had the Qur'an, but I often wondered where these other books could be found. I wanted to read what I had to believe in. There was no answer to that quest in any of the instruction I got in the mosque. However, surprisingly for me, that question was answered several years later when a Christian gave me my first Bible.

Pre-Islamic faith

My parents and community, though devoutly Muslim, also lived within the influences of centuries of pre-Islamic traditional culture and spirituality. For example, a thousand years ago, before Islam was accepted in Somalia, all Somalis believed in one God, the Creator, whom they referred to as *Waaq*. All blessings came from Waaq! The source of peace was also Waaq. As the indigenous residents of Bulo Burte embraced Islam, therefore, their context included pre-Islamic yearnings for peacemaking rooted in God and understood as a gift from God.

As I see it, significant aspects of the civil society that has long characterized Bulo Burte derives especially from the pre-Islamic heritage of peacemaking. For example, a well known pre-Islamic aphorism that helped form my peacemaking commitments stated, "Give your enemy fresh milk!" Members of my family line were recognized as peacemaking leaders. In later years that recognition was an asset in my role as a leader in peacemaking efforts when Somalia fell apart in inter-clan conflict. In that role I often counseled, "Give your enemy fresh milk!"

The pre-Islamic influence included Christian and Jewish beliefs and practices that contributed to the traditions of our community and family. Christian and Jewish influences were present throughout the Middle East at the time of Muhammad. Seventh-century Islam, springing forth from western Arabia,

overlaid Christian or Christianized societies. That was even true
in Arabia itself. In fact, the Qur'an mirrors a variety of Christian themes, including Jesus as the Messiah,[3] born of a virgin,
miracle worker, and the one without sin.

In Somalia too there are indications of pre-Islamic Christian
or Jewish influences. South Yemen in southern Arabia, across
the Gulf of Aden north of the Somali-inhabited Horn, was a
Christian kingdom. Ethiopia on the Somali western borderlands
was also Christian for several centuries before Muhammad
began his preaching in Mecca.

Among my people these Christian and Jewish influences were
interwoven with the Islam of my family. For example, whenever my father slew an animal, he would make the sign of the
cross on the lintel of the door into our home. Furthermore, the
burial site for my clan is marked with gravestones in the shape
of the cross. Especially remarkable to me was my mother's fre-
quent expression in prayer, "*Waaq iyo Ina Madi*" (In the name
of God and his only Son).

Every year Muslims join the annual pilgrimage to Mecca. At
the climax of the pilgrimage, they participate in the *Eid al-
Adha*, the feast of sacrifice. They are commemorating God's
provision of a ram as a substitutionary sacrifice to redeem a son
of Abraham from death. (They believe the son was Ishmael,
Jews and Christians believe it was Isaac.) In commemoration of
that sacrifice, Muslims on the pilgrimage as well as Muslims
around the world offer animal sacrifices.

In my home Father would select a newborn male and female
lamb a year before the Eid al-Adha. These needed to be spotless
and healthy. Then at the Eid he would slay these two lambs and
dab the blood on the lintel and posts of the door into our home.
This is most certainly a flashback to the Jewish Passover
described in Exodus.

The Eid was not the only time my father slew a lamb. In my
community and throughout Somalia, when a person becomes
ill, the religious leaders often kill a lamb and bathe the ill person in its blood. They believe that blood heals! Imagine my
astonishment to discover as a teenager that the blood of Jesus
cleanses us from all sin (1 John 1:7)!

Preparation for the gospel

After my father's death, my mother told of seeing visions of him living in a red house. Across the yard surrounding the house she saw the lambs he had sacrificed over the years, but they were now resurrected, living lambs. What did that mean? Is it possible that her visions were initiated by the Holy Spirit seeking to open the eyes of my family and my people to Jesus, the Lamb of God who was slain and resurrected for our redemption? In the book of Revelation the apostle John describes a vision of the slain lamb standing in the center of the throne of God (Revelation 5:6). That vision is a metaphor of Jesus crucified and risen.

I believe that the lambs my father sacrificed were a sign of Jesus, the Lamb of God who was crucified and who rose from the dead. The heritage that my family and community bequeathed to me was a preparation for my journey of coming home to Christ. By the time my mother's visions took place, I already believed in Jesus the Messiah; my father's sacrifice of lambs before my conversion nevertheless helped prepare me to believe in Jesus as the Lamb of God. In seminary I learned about redemptive analogies or paradigms. These are signs of the gospel within a culture.

This is not to say that such signs are the gospel. For example, when driving from Milwaukee to Minneapolis, I follow the road signs. But those signs are not the destination. If I would stop at a sign that says "Minneapolis," yet not continue on the road until I arrive at the destination the sign is pointing to, I would never arrive at Minneapolis. In the same way, there are multiple signs of the gospel within my traditional religious heritage and within Islam. However, these signs are not the salvation provided in Jesus the Messiah. The sacrifice of lambs in my home were important signs for me in my quest for wholeness, but I only knew salvation when I arrived in the presence of the One toward whom those signs pointed.

The dominant force within my heritage was Islam, and my mother embodied the essence of that faith. The Islam of my parents was not mixed up with folk religion and superstition. For example, most of my buddies wore leather talismans with portions of the Qur'an inscribed as good luck charms. Our family had none of this; we took seriously the warnings in the Qur'an against using the name of God magically. We understood the Qur'an to command us to use the name of God most reverently. For example, we were never to utter the name of God in the toilet.

To sum up, there were three significant strands forming my community and family: (1) traditional Somali faith and practice; (2) nuances of Christian and biblical faith and practice; and (3) Islam. Our religious heritage was like a three-strand rope. By the time I was born, the Islamic strand was the most significant. Nevertheless, the other two strands were also present. It was all three of these themes that contributed to opening my soul to a serious consideration of Jesus the Messiah as revealed in the Bible.

CHAPTER 2

From Islam to the Gospel
The Hospital and May 15 High School
(1968–72)

I am the way, the truth and the life.
—Jesus

WHEN I was fourteen I ventured boldly to Mogadishu 140 miles (225 kilometers) south of Bulo Burte for post-primary middle school. Mogadishu was our nation's capital, a sprawling, feisty metropolis of half a million people. I loved the dynamic pulse of the city.

Occasionally I came home for a brief school break. I enjoyed my mother's cooking, my father's wisdom, and the joviality of siblings. It was good drinking tangy camel's milk from our herd. I reveled in these occasional visits home.

Then on one of my visits fever struck me like a bolt of lightning; I contracted cerebral malaria. Alas, after a few days at home I had come to a precipice; the dark chasm of death was before me as malaria ravaged my mind and body. I was only fifteen; I felt too young to die!

I was admitted to the Sudan Interior Mission (SIM) Hospital in Bulo Burte. My spirit was touched by the generous kindness of the missionary nurses, and my fever abated as they administered modern medicines that attacked the malaria parasite that nearly snatched my life.

The Sudan Interior Mission

Fourteen years earlier in 1954 the SIM had negotiated an invitation to open medical and educational programs in Somalia. For some years a small SIM team had been based in Yemen just north of Somalia across the Gulf of Aden. Their special focus was praying for the doors to open in Somalia for SIM presence, service, and witness. God used political developments to bring about an answer to their prayers.

At the conclusion of World War II, Somalia became a trust territory of the United Nations with interim governments preparing the country for political independence in 1960. The north was under British authority and the south, Italian. Religious freedom was mandated in all United Nations trust territories. So in 1954 the interim authorities extended a welcome to SIM to begin educational and medical programs. A year later the small SIM team in Yemen moved to Mogadishu. Shortly after that, SIM opened a mission hospital in my hometown. By the providence of God that hospital saved my life. Another mission, Eastern Mennonite Missions (EMM), had also been invited to Somalia and was registered as Somalia Mennonite Mission (SMM).

Surprised by Joseph—cautious exploration of the Bible

As I recovered from the malaria, I asked a nurse from Australia for something to read that was appropriate for someone learning English. She gave me the narrative of Joseph from the Bible. I was delighted for it kindled memories of the boys of our town sitting in a circle listening to Imam Sheikh Rashid recount this rather obscure story from the Qur'an. I soon learned that the fuller account the nurse gave me was found in the Torah of Moses—one of the books I as a Muslim had to believe in yet had no idea where to find. I cannot exaggerate my excitement.

The seed of faith in biblical revelation was planted in my soul when I read the account of Joseph in the Torah. Imam Rashid referred to the Torah as the *Taurat* that God has revealed; I was so excited to have a portion of this book from God. After leaving the hospital, I continued reading the Bible, but gingerly. I believed that these Christians were most likely deceived infidels. The lore of the town was that Christians were polytheists. The Catholics worshipped Mary. All Christians worshipped Jesus whom they believed to be a god. I knew that giving God associates guaranteed that I would go to hell. Furthermore, friends warned me that Christians had changed and corrupted the Bible. I was concerned that the gracious SIM hospital team might deceive me and entice me to leave Islam. Yet for the next two years I cautiously read the Bible in private.

There were other powerful influences competing for my allegiance. I came home to Bulo Burte on most school breaks and those visits immersed me in my earlier life. However, in Mogadishu my studies at the May 15 High School had very little connection with my childhood memorization of the Qur'an. This fine school was named in recognition of the Somali Youth League (SYL), established on May 15, 1943, to lead Somalia to independence. That happened! The League was the political party that led Somalia to political independence on July 1, 1960.

The May 15 High School was built in 1969 by the European Common Market with the intention of equipping a young generation of leaders who would lead the way for Somali national development in the wake of political independence. I reveled in courses such as geography and political science, subjects that my Qur'anic studies had never explored. However, I was also troubled by the atheism in the school. We had Russian teachers who attempted to indoctrinate us with Marxist ideology.

In the midst of these ideological crosscurrents, I persisted in a personal reading and study of the Bible. The Holy Spirit was slowly and mysteriously opening my heart to believe in the message of the Bible. The journey to faith in Jesus the Messiah as my Savior, however, did not happen instantly. It was a two-year journey.

Jesus met me

During a school break at Bulo Burte, two years after my near-death malaria attack, I went to the home of Dr. Marc Erickson, who was in charge of the SIM hospital. He was from Milwaukee, Wisconsin, in the United States. He was an unusual kind of "doctor in charge" in our context because in the late afternoons he would be on the basketball court shooting hoops with the community youth. He would invite any of these emerging sportsmen to come to his home to read the Bible. Because of my weakened arm from that childhood donkey fall, I had never played basketball. However, I was curious about the doctor's invitation to the basketball players for a Bible study.

It was two years after my stay in the hospital that I boldly decided to ask to participate in a Bible study. Marc consented. The Bible study in his home, however, was illegal. By that time Somali law boldly stated that no one could teach Somalis any religion except the religion of Islam. Eight years earlier an overzealous imam had killed Merlin Grove, the director of the Somalia Mennonite Mission. The reason this self-appointed jihadist attacked was his consternation about Somalis becoming Christians. Although the attack happened at the SMM mission offices in Mogadishu, the attacker had hailed from Central Somalia, where I was from.

Marc and I both knew we were pushing legal boundaries, but we also knew that studying the Bible was preeminently important. Marc believed that Jesus Christ was his ultimate authority. Christ had commanded his followers to make disciples (Matthew 28:18-20), so Marc was committed to making disciples. The community appreciated Marc's medical ministry and consequently was willing to be flexible in applying the law.

Marc recalls the day when I first came to his house:

> Ahmed appeared with a friend at my door on a Sunday afternoon. They said, "We want to become Christians." They made it clear that they had come to follow Jesus and not to get anything from the good doctor. We discussed the dangers of confessing Christ. They had thought about that and said they would be secret believers. Because of the ever present informants, we responded cautiously to such requests. But I felt strangely moved to invite Ahmed and his friend to pray inviting Jesus to come and indwell them. Obviously Ahmed had been wrestling with God and his truth for a long time.

The first thing Marc did was invite me to pray that God would open my heart to the gospel. So Marc and I prayed that God would come into my heart and guide me to the truth. At that moment the Holy Spirit opened my heart to the truth of Jesus Christ. With eagerness I began the study of the Bible with Marc, not as a cautious observer, but as a believer. First he led me through the book of James, in the New Testament. So much in that book related to the themes of justice and righteousness that I had learned at the mosque from the imam as he taught the foundations of Islamic law. I was intrigued.

When I returned to Mogadishu, Marc introduced me to several of the SIM team members in Mogadishu: Howard Borlace, John Warner, and John Miller. Later I also met the Mennonites, whose center was around the corner from the SIM. Two older Mennonites became like aunts to me, Naomi Smoker and Bertha Beachy.

The SIM team's study of the Gospel of Luke and Acts enriched my understanding of Jesus Christ, the nature of salvation, and the life of the church. Every class was a new experience of discovery. Jesus amazed me! So did the life of the early church described in Acts. I felt at the depth of my being the tug of Jesus and the winsome attractiveness of the church as a fellowship of forgiveness and reconciliation.

Back home in Bulo Burte, on another of those breaks from school, Marc conducted a two-week Bible institute. We often met under the acacia trees whose shade protected us from the fierce heat of the sun. I attended these studies faithfully; neither Marc nor I missed a lesson. We studied 1 and 2 Peter. In that study the essence of the gospel gripped me. Recall how my father would sprinkle the blood of sacrificed lambs on the lintel and posts of the door of our home. Now I was amazed to read that Christ is the fulfillment of the quest for forgiveness and protection that my father sought in those sacrificed lambs:

> For you know that it was not with perishable things such as silver or gold that you were redeemed from the empty way of life handed down to you from your forefathers, but with the precious blood of Christ, a lamb without blemish or defect. He was chosen before the foundation of

the world, but was revealed in these last times for your
sake. (1 Peter 1:18-20)

Then in the very next chapter we read about the church.

But you are a chosen people, a royal priesthood, a holy
nation, a people belonging to God, that you may declare
the praises of him who called you out of darkness into his
wonderful light. Once you were not a people, but now
you are the people of God; once you had not received
mercy, but now you have received mercy. (1 Peter 2:9-10)

These Bible studies helped to give me a solid foundation in
the New Testament's revelation in regard to Jesus Christ. After
we had completed the Peter studies, we went on to study 1, 2,
and 3 John. Then we studied the book of Hebrews, which was
relevant to the rather mystical Sufi Islam that prevailed in central Somalia. With its emphasis on sacrifice and high priests,
Hebrews was remarkable for me, who had grown up in a home
where animal sacrifices were regularly practiced for our protection and forgiveness. I gained deeper insights into the mystery of
the atonement centered in the sacrificial self-giving of Jesus, the
Lamb of God, for our forgiveness and redemption.

The day in Marc's home when we prayed together for the
Holy Spirit to reveal Jesus Christ to me has been the most
important day of my life. Although I did not fully understand
what it meant to believe in and follow Jesus, I knew that I had
begun a journey of incredible challenge and purpose. That is the
day I truly came home! The subsequent Bible studies introduced
me to more about the Jesus who had touched me.

Coming home

When I believed in Christ, so much became clear. I knew where
I had come from and where I was going. I knew that in Jesus
and the church I had indeed come home. Many of my friends
have experienced destructive lives. I believe this is because they
have never found their true home. But that day in prayer with
Marc Erickson, I knew that Christ and the church fulfilled the

yearnings that were planted within my soul by my Muslim family and by the Muslim faith and socialization that had surrounded me the first seventeen years of my life.

As a Muslim I really wanted to know God. In Jesus I met God as my loving heavenly father. I yearned for the assurance that my sins were forgiven. In Jesus I knew my sins were forgiven. I longed for assurance of eternal salvation and now in Jesus I knew that heaven was my destiny. I am grateful for the ways Islam prepared me to hear and believe in Christ (Galatians 3:23-24).

Paul writes in his letter to the Romans, "Since we have been justified through faith, we have peace with God through our Lord Jesus Christ" (Romans 5:1). As a boy studying Islam in the local mosque, I had developed a commitment to faithfully doing my obligatory salat five times daily. I believed that angels, perched on each of my two shoulders, kept account of what was on the debit and credit side of my balance scales. However, in Jesus Christ the balance scales is no more, for Jesus has taken our place. Through faith in Jesus we receive the gift of forgiveness. This was a tremendous relief for me, a mid-teenage lad who sincerely sought for God and his peace.

The church like a nomadic home

All nomadic Somalis have lived in houses that move whenever the family moves. That has also been the story of my life. I was already a wanderer before I met Christ, going back and forth from Mogadishu to Bulo Burte, and spending a prolonged period in Johar during the great famine. But ever since that day when I believed in Christ, I have come home. This home is not stationary. Like the nomadic huts, my home is often on the move. But wherever and whatever the circumstances, dusty drought or luscious pastures, when I met Christ I knew that he is the door into my true home.

That true home is the church. It is like a nomadic hut. The hut has ribbing and a center pole. The center pole is the *udub*. The matting of the roof is woven reeds. It is the *tol* (weave).

The udub is Christ crucified and risen. He is the center and the whole house is supported by him. The pole is analogous to

the cross where Jesus gave his life as our living sacrifice on the cross. Christ crucified and risen is the Creator and Sustainer of the church.

We who believe are the ribbing. All the ribbing comes together at the apex of the udub. All the ribs are held together, anchored and supported by meeting each other at the top. Any ribbing that is not anchored to the center pole is useless.

We are also the tol, the woven mat that is thrown over the ribbing to provide a protective roof. The Holy Spirit weaves us together in the bonds of love. The tol can also be a metaphor of the grace of Christ; so we are woven together in the grace and love of Christ who is our righteousness, our covering.

That day when I believed in and committed my life to Jesus Christ, I became a rib in the house of God, the church. That is my home, now and eternally. I have never walked with Jesus Christ alone. That would be like a rib attempting to stand upward alone or providing solitary support for the woven mat covering; that is impossible. We must always live within the fellowship of the church. In my commitment to Christ, the Holy Spirit binds me to all the other ribs and I am woven together with all the other reeds that provide a covering for the house. Within that house I revel in the secure covering of the grace of Christ.

The mosque and the church

Although my Muslim roots prepared me to seek the gospel, my Muslim heritage is not the gospel. Neither is the mosque the church. For this reason when the Holy Spirit called me and I confessed faith in Jesus Christ, it became immediately clear to me that the mosque and the church do not mix. So I never returned to the mosque for prayers after my conversion. I knew that the Muslim home is supported by another center pole, namely the Qur'an.

I recognize that some of my friends continue in both worlds after believing in Christ. They try to keep a foot in both communities, the mosque and the church. I do not condemn them. Some tell me that when they participate in both, doors open for them to share the gospel. But if I speak my convictions about this, I think that these believers struggle with a confusing identity, both personally as well as in their relationship with the Muslim community. To attempt to live within both the mosque and the church creates a homeless mind. I believe it is important to be clear about our true home and identity. For this reason, from the day Jesus met me, my home has been the church, and Jesus alone is my udub.

Baptism

In the Bible studies in Mogadishu, I learned that disciples of Jesus are baptized. I wanted to follow Jesus all the way, not half-heartedly. I knew well that in the Somali Islamic culture baptism was considered the point of no return and could bring reprisals such as family alienation, or even death threats. Yet I wanted to give testimony to the clarity of my commitment to believe in and follow Jesus. So, some months after that day in 1971 in Bulo

Burte when I found my true home, a friend and I requested baptism. We slipped out of the SIM center in Mogadishu early in the morning when it was still dark, just as the cacophonies of the first prayer call were echoing throughout the city. Three SIM missionaries accompanied us and at least one Somali brother. We were baptized in the Indian Ocean east of the Lido beach in the Karaan section of Mogadishu.

On the day I was baptized I confessed in the presence of God and others my commitment to believe in and follow Jesus Christ in the fellowship of the church; I have never looked back.

CHAPTER 3

Christ or Success
Nairobi
(1973–74)

*The Lord is my Shepherd,
I shall not be in want.*
—Psalms

M Y baptism vows were the seal on my commitment to know and follow Christ for the rest of my life. To use the words of Jesus, I put my hand to the plow, and I have not looked back (Galatians 1:17-18). However, this is not to say that I did not have deep and sometimes disturbing times of counting the cost of that commitment.

The immediate challenge following my baptism was how to relate to Somalia's Marxist revolution that had taken place just two years earlier. The revolution occurred on October 21, 1969, when the military assassinated President Abdirashid Ali Sharmarke. Prior to that, Somali politics were corrupt but dynamic. Somalis practiced and loved their clan-based democracy. Prime ministers had come and gone in the rough and tumble of post-independence politics. Even presidential leadership changed through the ballot box. The boisterous conversations in the tea shops across the country were about current debates in Parliament. Somali representative democracy had been rambunctiously participatory.

Then our October Revolution changed all that. General Mohamed Siad Barre—supported by the military with strong backing from the Soviet Union—initiated a Marxist revolution. Somalia was pressed into the mold of a Soviet satellite. As the revolution took its course most institutions were nationalized. By 1972 the government had even taken over the properties of Sudan Interior Mission (SIM) and Somalia Mennonite Mission (SMM). This was the second major crisis to challenge the SIM and SMM. The first was in 1964, five years before the 1969 revolution. At that time both the SIM and SMM were confronted with a perplexing dilemma. The government of the recently independent Somalia required that Arabic and Islam be taught in the mission schools, while at the same time prohibiting the propagation of any religion except Islam. The government promised to provide the teachers for the Islamic syllabus. What should the SIM and SMM do? By that time there were small clusters of Somali believers in Jesus the Messiah, and they were quite ready to share their counsel with the two missions. Although there were different opinions, I am told that many counseled the missions to accept the government requirement. They counseled that this would contribute to trust-building. Somali believers observed that the Holy Spirit was not bound by circumstances and the gospel is the power of God. Hence, the missions did not need to fear or resist restrictions.

As the decision unfolded SIM and SMM took different paths. SIM closed their education program, including their school in Bulo Burte, focusing instead on medical ministries. SMM decided to cooperate with the government; consequently the SMM education program expanded vigorously and eventually included an excellent high school, Shebelli Secondary School.

By the time of the 1972 nationalization, the SIM team had been significantly reduced. In 1973, a year after nationalization, the SIM withdrew for a period of time. However, SMM had forty missionaries, most of whom were reassigned to government-administered institutions. SMM hoped to continue with their people serving in government programs. However, the authorities required a gradual reduction in SMM personnel. Four years later, in 1976, the government thanked the SMM for their service and requested that all missionaries leave. It was the atheistic revolutionaries, not the Muslims, who demanded that the Somalia Mennonite Mission leave Somalia, as the Sudan

Interior Mission had done earlier. I was baptized at a time when political forces were challenging the presence in Somalia of both the SIM and SMM. These were indeed revolutionary times.

Rejecting the Marxist option

The revolution needed officers and leaders who were committed to the communist ideology. Consequently scholarships for studies in Marxist universities in Eastern Europe or the Soviet Union abounded. As soon as they graduated from high school many of my friends were offered these scholarships. My best friend got a scholarship and off to East Germany he went. I was eager to follow him.

However, the developing revolution troubled me. General Mohammed Siad Barre was called "our victorious father." Songs were sung everywhere that called him *guul wade said* (the father of all knowing). This was idolatry. Only God was all knowing. I struggled immensely.

Then a delegation arrived in central Mogadishu from Almaty, Kazakhstan, one of the Central Asian Republics of the Soviet Union. At a mass rally the delegation sang about Lenin for us Somalis. Christians sing that Jesus lives. This Kazakhstan delegation took the tune of a Christian song about the resurrection of Jesus entitled "He Lives," but instead of Christ they substituted the name of Lenin. I was appalled! Lenin was the mastermind of the Communist Revolution that formed the Soviet Union; he had died half a century earlier. Yet they sang that Lenin, not Christ, lives! I was deeply grieved.

From all that we high school students could see, the road to success, prestige, and secure employment in revolutionary Somalia was to accept an East German scholarship. But I knew that I could not follow both loyalties—commitment to Christ and commitment to Siad Barre's Marxism. For me the choice seemed clear: success or Christ. I decided to abandon my goals of financial and employment security. I made an irrevocable decision not to accept an East German scholarship. I would leave Somalia, not for East Germany, but for Kenya to the south.

I hoped that Kenya would provide an opportunity to further clarify my journey with Christ. Although I knew I had come home when I met Christ, I was still struggling with fundamental questions about the meaning of Christ and the church. Like Paul, who invested three years in Arabia thinking through the meaning of his conversion (Galatians 1:17-18), I needed a space to contemplate the meaning of my encounter with Christ.

Within my Muslim worldview, God is utterly transcendent and sovereign. It is for this reason that in Islam there can be no incarnation (God becoming fully human in Christ) and no cross (Christ suffering and dying). My Muslim worldview insisted that the incarnation and the cross were impossible compromises of God's sovereignty and power; yet the incarnation and the cross are the soul of the gospel. I needed time away from my people to think through the radical transformation in my theological assumptions that the gospel demanded. I would do that in Kenya, far from home and the colliding cross currents of Marxism and Islam. I had friends in Kenya; surely they would receive me.

Before leaving Somalia, I made a farewell journey to Bulo Burte, my beloved dusty village. I shared my plans to go to Kenya with my father and mother. I had a good relationship with my parents. When I was in my mid-teens my father learned that I had become a believer in Jesus the Messiah. When town elders chided my father for not rebuking me for this, he always defended my commitment to Christ. Some years later when I returned to Somalia and served with a number of Christian philanthropic programs, clan leaders pressed my father to take strong actions against me. But as far as I know my father was always my best defender. He would make wry comments to the detractors, "So your sons are very good Muslims, are they? How often are they at prayers? And what are they doing to help uplift the community? Look at the good my son is doing before you criticize him for his faith."

I was grateful for my father's support of my decision to follow Christ, and I yearned for his blessing on my decision to go to Kenya. More than that, I also needed his financial support. So I presented a quite embarrassing request to my father, "Please give me my inheritance now." Inheritance is distributed when the father dies. I knew that my request could seem inappropriate and presumptuous.

Fortunately, my father gently put me at ease. As always, his generosity astonished me. In his measured voice—which I had come to respect highly—he replied, "I will not give you your inheritance at this time. Neither will I loan you money. Rather I will give you a gift of 500 Somali shillings. Furthermore, I give you my wholehearted blessing! My son, your decision to go to Kenya is the right choice. You have decided not to go to East Germany; that is a wise decision. In the future, if you return home from your travels, there will be ample time to apportion inheritance to you and all my children."

The trek to Kenya

Leaving home with my father's blessing and financial support was enormously freeing and encouraging. My heart overflowed with thanksgiving; this was an answer to prayer from my Father in heaven!

Back in Mogadishu, I quietly said goodbye to friends and the church. That was a momentous day; Somalia had been my home for the last twenty years. On July 4, 1973, I left for Kenya. I mounted a freight truck for what would be a fourteen-day trek, traversing some 1,000 miles (1600 kilometers) over poorly maintained tracks across the acacia scrublands of southwest Somalia and northeast Kenya.

The remote El Waaq-Mandera border crossing into Kenya was tricky. I had no legal documents. So some distance from the border I dismounted the truck and had to walk alone for many miles through the acacia scrubbrush.

To sustain my hope, I was encouraged by Psalm 23. This psalm describes the Lord as my Good Shepherd—my Companion, Savior, and Guide in the perilous journey that I had begun. I felt no need or desire for the magical power of talismans with portions of the Qur'an. These magical powers had no allure because I knew the Good Shepherd personally. I was encouraged as I recited from the Shepherd's psalm: "Even though I walk through the valley of the shadow of death, I will fear no evil, for you are with me; your rod and staff, they comfort me. You prepare a table before me, in the presence of my enemies" (Psalm 23:4-5). I knew that discovery and arrest would end my sojourn with possible life-threatening consequences. Yet even in the valley of death, God was there.

Somehow on this trek on foot at the border, my possessions vanished, including my Bible. I do not know how that could have happened, but they were probably taken when I was napping. The loss of my possessions was a warning as to how precarious my situation was. Yet I refused to succumb to fear as I reaffirmed, "The Lord is my Shepherd!"

The truck driver picked me up again some distance into Kenya. At other hamlets along the road where there were police checkpoints, I would resume the trek by foot for some miles and then would rendezvous with the truck far beyond the checkpoint. In Wajir, in the heart of the Somali-inhabited regions of northeastern Kenya, the trucker took me into his home overnight, but warned that I must not talk with anyone for my central Somalia accent would betray me.

Finally on July 18, 1973, at 9:00 p.m., I alighted from the truck at Sixteenth Street in Eastleigh, Nairobi. Right there was my dear friend Ardon! Indeed the Lord was my Shepherd protecting me all the way.

I asked Ardon, "Where do David and Grace Shenk and Ron and Rufus Hartzler live?"

The Shenks and Hartzlers were among the first Mennonite missionaries who had to leave Somalia when the nationalization began in 1972. These families had moved into the Eastleigh area of Nairobi in order to continue their commitments to serving the Somali people. It was densely inhabited by Somalis and was a significant communication and travel crossroads for Somalis in northeast Africa. Ardon took me to the apartments where the Shenks and Hartzlers lived. It was late evening so they were astonished to see me, but welcomed me with utmost hospitality. I stayed in the Shenk home overnight.

I had 180 shillings remaining of the 500 shillings my father had given me for the trip to Kenya. The trip had cost me 320 shillings. I thanked God for loving care, including adequate provision!

The church in Eastleigh

For over a year the Eastleigh section of Nairobi was my home. The Mennonites had rented a five-apartment complex on Eighth Street in Eastleigh intending to develop the facility into a community center. In the meantime they had opened a reading room and library. One two-room apartment was home for about half a dozen Somali brothers who had come to Kenya just as I had done. We spread our mats and slept on the floor at night and were engaged in various activities at the center during the day.

The Mennonite team members who were exiled from Somalia were beginning a church that would attract scattered Mennonites from Kenya and Tanzania who had migrated to Nairobi. Having been born in Tanzania, David knew Swahili, and he served as pastor of that Swahili-speaking fellowship. The congregation met a couple of miles across town in a hall known as Avon. I immediately joined fully with this fellowship. Although I was the only Somali who attended this church, I often joined the Shenk children and their Kenyan friends from our street on the forty-five minute walk to church. This was unusual, for Somalis intermingle cautiously with other ethnic groups. Although the experience was new for me, I enjoyed the multi-ethnic fellowship. Soon I was chosen treasurer of that church. I learned enough Swahili to get along.

Another fellowship was also developing within the Eighth Street complex—a group of Somali believers. I immersed myself in that fellowship as well. We met Friday mornings in our Eastleigh residence. Our vision was to establish a thriving fellowship of Somali believers in the city. That fellowship went through a lot of transitions, ups and downs, and it has not always been continuous. Twenty years later, however, I returned to Nairobi with my family and served as a leader in a developing thriving fellowship of Somali believers. The Lord had indeed prospered our original vision in Eastleigh two decades earlier.

No matter how few or many believers there were over the years, there was always a persistent vision for a Somali-speaking church to emerge in Nairobi. Consistent with that vision, during the 1970s the Nairobi Mennonite Church with Eastern Mennonite Missions developed the Eighth Street center into a multi-ministry facility known as the Eastleigh Fellowship Center. It took a decade to develop the center and the service ministries of the center. Today, a thousand people a week, including hundreds of Somalis, use that center. It is located at a significant communication crossroads for the Somali people of northeastern and eastern Africa.

The Nairobi Mennonite Church that met several miles from Eastleigh was my first experience in a church where local families worshipped together. In Somalia Christians had worshipped unobtrusively in small groups composed of young men. There were only a few Somali women believers, and children could not attend. (An exception was a Bantu congregation in southern Somalia with historical ties to Kenya.) This is to say that there were no Somali Christian families. Of course, the Muslim worship gatherings in my community had never included families either. The emerging church in Somalia was not able to move beyond the Muslim expectation that men and women not meet together in worship. Although our fellowships were tolerated within Islamic Somalia, the legality of their existence was always questionable. In Eastleigh, however, we were very openly church. I enjoyed immensely the religious freedoms of Kenya.

Sunday evenings I worshipped with the Nairobi Pentecostal Church. Imagine my astonishment when I first attended this church. Here, hundreds of families worshipped together! A thousand men, women, and children gathered for worship in the same sanctuary! The Canadian pastor, Mervyn Thomas, preached powerful biblical sermons; I had never heard such preaching. Miracles of healing and transformed lives were a normal expectation in the weekly worship.

I thus immersed myself in these three streams of Christian spirituality: East African Mennonite, Somali with Muslim background, and exuberant Pentecostal. Mosque gatherings tend to be uniform all over the world; their ritual prayers are the same. Yet in Nairobi I discovered that the church is richly diverse. I reveled in these fascinating expressions of the church of Jesus Christ.

Opportunities to serve

Our center on Eighth Street was across the street and about a hundred yards from the mosque on the corner. We developed good relations with the mosque congregation. Occasionally we had the leaders over to our center for meals and dialogues. That fraternity helped to provide acceptance for the emergence of a Somali fellowship of Christian believers, all of whom came from Muslim background. At that time the mosque was Sufi, a mystical stream of Islam that is often quite open to people of other faiths. The Sufi movement is a quest to experience God; traditional Islam focuses on submission to the will of God, but not on experiencing God. Sufis are often intrigued with the gospel, for indeed Jesus and the ministry of the Holy Spirit fulfill the yearnings of Sufi spirituality. Sufi communities are often recognized as communities of peace. Our center was the presence of a community of peace centered in Christ. The Sufi community focused on mystical spirituality; we were a community empowered by the Holy Spirit to serve the wider community in a variety of ministries.

During the thirteen months that I lived there, the center on Eighth Street provided opportunity to serve in a variety of ways. I did not while away my free time on the streets; instead I volunteered my evenings supervising the library. I did everything I could to be helpful. The center's ministries were touching hundreds of students; the reading room and library were especially appreciated by students who could find no quiet place for study in their congested homes where a dozen people might live and sleep in a small one-room apartment. In addition to these commitments to service, I plunged into academics at the Central High School.

At this time I also participated in a team—led by David Shenk—that developed a Bible study course for Muslims. Recall my observation that Islam prepared me to believe the gospel. We carried that conviction into developing the course, which was a narrative study of the Bible beginning with Genesis 1 and concluding with the climax of history as described in Revelation 21 and 22, the last two chapters of the Bible. Wherever we felt that the Qur'an and Islam had signs of the gospel that were pertinent to the biblical narrative, we elaborated upon those signs. For example, we affirmed the conviction in Islam that Jesus is the Messiah and that the Torah is the word of God. We built upon those same themes within Islam that helped to open my heart to the gospel some years before in Bulo Burte.

We called this course *The People of God*. After the first draft was completed, we asked Muslim friends to evaluate the course for us. We took their advice seriously and revised it in light of their counsel. When the course was finally released in English, Swahili, and Somali, we were astonished by the interest. For some years, over a thousand enrolled annually and went on to complete the four-booklet series. Others in far-off countries carried forward the vision, and today this course is available in some forty-five languages around the world. As far as I know, Muslims have never objected to this course, for it communicates Christ in ways that present the gospel as good news for Muslims. My wife, Martha, and I have each used this course with Muslims; it has given great joy to see the Holy Spirit using the studies to open people's hearts to Jesus the Messiah and to the gift of salvation that Jesus offers.

I did all these engagements as a volunteer because I wanted to serve Jesus. But I did need food and lodging. Happily the center did provide a place to stay. Amazingly, my food allowance came from a church in Chicago known as Reba Place. When they learned about me, they decided to provide a monthly stipend that was just enough to keep me fed with a few extra shillings for miscellaneous expenses. This was a remarkable affirmation that indeed Jesus was my Good Shepherd.

Discouragement and renewal

In the midst of all this activity, however, I was lonely. This was my first extensive time away from home. I was twenty years old. Most of my friends had gone to East Germany and some were returning to Somalia with good and prestigious jobs. I went through a deep valley of discouragement. I pondered why it was that following Christ had brought me to a dead end. Half a block from the center, Eighth Street became a dead end; it was a metaphor for the dead end that was before me in my life. It was becoming increasingly evident that for me, following Christ meant abandoning educational, professional, and financial success. Eastleigh was a dead end street for me!

On one occasion I met several men from my own clan. I was delighted. As my fellow clansmen surely they would provide companionship for me, I thought. I knew that many destitute Somalis who had come to Nairobi sought out and clung to relatives or acquaintances for their basic living costs. So I assured my fellow clansmen that I did not want any financial help; we could hang out together. But in surly response, they rebuked me for my commitment to Christ with less than veiled threats against me.[1] Their rejection was a blessing, however, for it meant I had no one to hang out with on the streets. Hence, I was saved from the temptations that so many Somalis succumbed to in the decadent slums of Eastleigh. For young men far from home, women, alcohol, and drugs were persistent temptations. Some acquired fast money through smuggling; others invested their days in idle loitering. The Lord preserved me from such slippery slopes.

Then friends arranged for me to attend the Word of Life Camp outside Nairobi. Here I met many Kenyan young people who loved the Lord. That was important. But most significant were the Bible studies based on Philippians. The Holy Spirit opened my soul to hear and receive the astounding worldview described in Philippians 2:1-11. That revelation transformed my own worldview. This study of Philippians was so important that I will linger on its significance. The main points were the following:

- First, I am to consider others better than myself (2:3).
- Second, I am to look out for the interests of others (2:4).
- Third, I am to have the spirit of Christ who humbled himself to become a servant (2:6-7).
- Fourth, Christ is God in human form who served in humility and who was crucified (2:6-8).
- Fifth, Christ is our risen Lord who has all authority (2:9-11).
- Sixth, my heritage is nothing in comparison to my heritage in Christ (3:4-8).

These principles were radically different from everything that had characterized my Muslim value and belief system. At the time Somalia was slowly sinking into the abyss of inter-clan conflict. The social capital of traditional and Islamic society was eroding. Neither our Muslim tradition nor our pre-Islamic traditions were able to stem the slow movement toward disintegration. But here in Philippians I met a Christ-centered faith and worldview that was truly transformative. What would happen if clans honored rival clans more than they honored themselves? What if people were ready to die for the enemy rather than seek to dominate the enemy? The seed of my peacemaking ministry of later years was planted in my soul during those Bible studies.

I discovered that I was very much like the apostle Paul in that I also had a wonderful heritage and clan genealogy. But my enviable heritage could not offer salvation to my people. Meeting Jesus meant counting my proud heritage as rubbish because Christ is so supremely wonderful when compared with anything I could offer.

The test of these commitments came much sooner than I anticipated. Back in my nook in Eastleigh, an acquaintance from Somalia appeared. He was from a rival clan. In fact, my clansmen considered themselves quite superior to his clan. My visitor, whom I continue to meet from time to time, often comments that he was astonished that I gave him my bed, while I slept on the floor. I did that not by constraint, but with joy.

Islam and the gospel

That Philippians Bible study clarified for me that there is a fundamental divide between Islam and the gospel, and the cross is at the center of it. In Islam God never suffers for us. Muslims believe Jesus is the miracle-working Messiah; he is not a Messiah who comes as the suffering servant described in Philippians. That is why Muslims believe that the crucifixion of Jesus is impossible—certainly not the power of God for all who believe, as Paul wrote to the Corinthians (1 Corinthians 1:18-25). Muslims, like the first-century Jews and Greeks who found the cross to be foolishness or a stumbling block, believe that the cross is weakness, certainly not power.

Islam objects to the cross because God is sovereign and never affected by our sin. So the cross is considered to be impossible. Muslims believe that the crucifixion of Jesus as described in the New Testament is an illusion; God rescued Jesus from the cross. Therefore, Islam misses the reconciliation offered in the cross. Islam misses redemption and assurance of forgiveness of sins. Islam misses the triumph of Christ crucified and risen over all the powers. Islam has not comprehended that God so loves us that he enters our sinful world as the Suffering Servant (Philippians 2:1-8), as the Good Shepherd who seeks the lost sheep (Luke 15:1-7) and who lays down his life for the sheep (John10:1-15).

Even though there are many hints within Islam that did help me to consider the gospel, the Muslim faith turns away from the cross. A Lebanese Muslim theologian, Tarif Khalidi, comments that although Muslims love Jesus, the Jesus of Islamic devotion leans away from the cross, whereas the Jesus of the gospels leans forward to the cross; in the gospel his life and mission are centered on the cross and resurrection.[2]

Following the Philippians Bible study, I strained forward to know Christ better. Living in the urban deserts of Eastleigh, I was no longer depressed, for Christ had touched me anew. I knew where I had come from and where I was going. I was a disciple of Jesus committed to following him wherever he might lead me. I was at peace about having relinquished the opportunity for studies in East Germany. I knew the Lord had led me to Eastleigh rather than East Germany. Christ was a far greater treasure than so-called success.

Somali political impasse deepens

Although I was a thousand miles from home, I was quite aware that the political order was under considerable stress in Somalia. A central issue in the early discontent was women's rights. The humanism of the Marxist government collided sharply with the Islam of the theologians in many ways, but especially in regard to women's rights. All through 1974 the conflict simmered. Then in 1975 the tensions exploded. On March 8, the worldwide women's day, President Siad Barre ordered that women and men would henceforth be equal in Somalia. The government ordered that a family inheritance must be divided equally among daughters and sons when the father died. A number of sheikhs protested saying that in the Qur'an women have different roles than men and inheritance laws are an example of this differentiation. In his rejoinder the President stated that the Qur'an is an old book that is out of date.

Islamist leaders led out in an explosion of opposition; eleven sheikhs were killed by government authorities. As this was happening Somali Air Force fighter jets collided over Mogadishu crashing into a residential area, killing many people. Many of the Muslim faithful believed the crash of the jets was the judgment of God upon the Marxist regime. The cycle of reprisals slowly began to accelerate. However, it is remarkable that the Barre regime managed to hold on for another seventeen years; the final collapse did not happen until 1991.

Eastleigh was like a calm island hundreds of miles from the political challenges that Somalia was struggling with. Yet we were also affected. I was deeply saddened when several of the Somali brothers in our believers' fellowship felt so deeply about the political challenges in Somalia that they joined the front lines with one military faction or another. Several of these dear brothers were killed in conflicts.

As for me, I believed that the only healing hope for my nation was the redemptive love of Christ, not violent conflict. Increasingly my prayer and hope were that the Lord would open the door for me to bear witness to the love of Christ among my people. I prayed that the Lord would provide a way for me to broaden my understanding and skills through further formal education. Although it seemed an impossible aspiration, I hoped that Eastleigh would become a stepping stone for study abroad. There was so much I wanted to explore using the mind God had given me.

Off to Oregon

As I prayed and waited for the next step to become clear for me, I did my best to invest my days fruitfully in congested Eastleigh by volunteering my evenings in the reading room and in further studies in Central High School. Then a series of amazing developments happened. I acquired a scholarship to go to Western Mennonite High School in Oregon. My problem with documents, which until now had obstructed any possibility of leaving Kenya, was rectified. Several friends and churches offered finances for the air tickets. Ron and Rufus Hartzler played a key role in arranging the finances for my sojourn to the United States for study.

My earlier decision to leave Somalia for Kenya had seemed to close the door on my aspirations for financial, educational, and professional success. By not accepting an East German scholarship, it seemed I had turned away from an open door that offered real opportunities. So this surprising open door to study in the United States amazed me. Jesus promised that those who leave family and land for his sake will receive a hundred times what they have sacrificed as well as eternal life. Indeed that promise was being fulfilled for me (Matthew 19:29).

So on August 26, 1974, at 10:00 a.m., just over thirteen months after arriving in Nairobi, I went to Embakasi Airport and boarded a DC 8, KLM flight for Amsterdam via Entebbe, Uganda, and Munich, Germany. I was very excited; this was my first plane ride. I was astonished as this powerful bird lifted off the Nairobi runway. I was amazed looking down on the clouds and the earth from seven miles up in the sky. This was, frankly, a miracle. God had taken me from Bulo Burte in central Somalia and was placing me in Oregon, in the United States!

CHAPTER 4

Pursuing Education
The American Academy
(1974–82)

If you are hosted by people with only one eye,
then become a one-eyed person.
—Somali Proverb

JUST over a decade earlier I had been a boy pestering donkeys while herding cattle and goats for my mother in Bulo Burte in central Somalia. Now I was flying to Amsterdam on my way to Western Mennonite High School in Oregon, in the United States, with a stop in Chicago. I had to change planes in Amsterdam to go to Chicago. But I had no awareness of time zone changes so I missed my plane to Chicago and had to sleep in Schiphol Airport, Amsterdam.

When I arrived in Chicago, Bob Guth met me. He took me to Evanston, Illinois, and the Reba Place Fellowship. In some ways this group reminded me of the Somali fellowship in Eastleigh, only it was much larger. Reba Place was a community of disciples of Jesus who believed that the first church described in Acts—where believers shared their possessions with one another—should be normal church life (Acts 2:42-47). In the Eastleigh Somali fellowship we had also shared generously with each other.

Although no one at Reba Place had ever met me, when they heard about my decision to leave Somalia rather than go to East Germany for school, they decided to assist me for study at Western Mennonite High School. A church in the Franconia Conference of the Mennonite Church assisted with the air ticket. This practical network of support for me, whom they had never met, was another revelation that the Lord is indeed my Shepherd and therefore I lack nothing!

I told my Reba Place hosts that I would like to meet with my friend Marc Erickson, who had led me to faith in Christ in Bulo Burte and now lived in Milwaukee, Wisconsin. At first they could not find his name in the phone book, so I told them his middle initial. That did it! Soon I was on a bus to Milwaukee.

Marc was being ordained that weekend at Elmbrook Church in Brookfield, Wisconsin, and I was there for that blessed event. When Dr. Eric Erickson and Nancy had returned from Somalia, he had become increasingly engaged at Elmbrook Church with a special focus on college and career-age young adults. A well known author, Stuart Briscoe, was lead pastor; he became a mentor to Marc and Nancy. About a decade later, in the 1980s, the Elmbrook Church began planting sister congregations, including Eastbrook in Glendale north of Milwaukee. Marc was a key leader in the Eastbrook Church.

In 1986, at the request of the church, he left his medical practice to give full time to planting and serving as pastor of this growing, thriving, missions-committed congregation. It was a joyous time, meeting my mentor and friend whose life and witness had winsomely commended Christ to me as a seventeen-year-old in Bulo Burte five years earlier.

Bidding farewell to the Ericksons, I resumed my journey to Portland and then to Salem, Oregon. At the airport I met my friend Ardon! Just as he was the first person I met in Eastleigh, he was now the first to meet me in Salem. He had arrived for studies at Western Mennonite High School just before I did. It was so good that we two friends could share together in getting used to American culture!

Western Mennonite High School

I reveled in my classes at WMHS. Especially helpful were my introductory courses on the Old Testament and New Testament. A year before, *The People of God* team in Nairobi had introduced me to the Bible as the narrative of God's saving love. Now my Bible studies were taking me into deeper understanding of the story. I discovered the drama of redemption beginning with Adam and Eve in the Garden (Genesis 1–3) and ending with consummation at the end of time, in the heavenly city that God is building (Revelation 21–22). The Qur'an, by contrast, is not a history; it is instruction on what people should believe and do. There are some intriguing allusions to history in the Qur'an, but it does not have the unifying thread of salvation history that the Bible does. Understanding this was a transformation for me and greatly deepened my appreciation for the relevance of the Bible to the real life challenges of modern society.

I related well to both faculty and students, and I studied faithfully. My English class gave me a solid foundation in the language I would use for academic study and international engagements. I also studied courses like algebra and biology. A highlight was a biology field trip into the deserts. Exploring and camping with the students energized me.

Glen Roth was a teacher and the principal of the school. He had served with the Mennonites in Somalia. On one occasion, when a student called me a "nigger," Glen was most angry and was ready to expel the student. But I asked him just to admonish the student and to forgive him.

On some occasions students did things that quite shocked me. For example, the guys put a light at the fountain in the center of the campus, opposite the women's dormitory. Sometimes at night they would go to the fountain and dance around the fountain in their underwear. My Muslim heritage strongly emphasizes modesty. In fact, at age twelve I stopped wearing short pants. I was disturbed that Christian youth would act in such an undignified manner. A more constructive bit of mischief, I felt, was when the guys would all sneak out of their dorm early in the morning to find breakfast in town nearby. Then, at breakfast time the girls would discover that there were no guys around.

The diet was also interesting. One teacher had me in his home and said that they would serve me rabbit for dinner.

I asked, "What does rabbit taste like?"

He said, "Chicken."

Later, when we were on a field trip, a teacher said he wanted to treat me to rattlesnake steak.

I asked, "What does rattlesnake taste like?"

He said, "Chicken."

So I discovered that for these Americans all meat that is not beef tastes like chicken. Even so, I ate with thanksgiving whatever people served me, although eating pork was a tremendous stretch. Like the Old Testament, the Qur'an absolutely condemns eating pork as utterly unclean. Pork was not a normal part of my diet!

I thrived at Western Mennonite High School. I developed enduring friendships with students and faculty. The Mennonite church on campus became my spiritual home. The student chapel delighted me, for I saw young people giving leadership to their campus church. This was the first time I had interacted with a sizeable community of young people who were committed to Jesus Christ.

Crediting my three years at May 15 High School in Mogadishu and my year at Central High School in Nairobi, WMHS granted me a high school diploma after completing my senior year. So in the fall of 1975, I enrolled as a freshman at Goshen College, in Goshen, Indiana, a four-year accredited liberal arts school supported by the Mennonite Church. Marcus Lind, one of my WMHS teachers and pastor of the Western Mennonite Church that met on campus, drove me the 2,400 miles to Goshen! His brother Wilbert had been the first leader of the Somalia Mennonite Mission.

Marcus urged me to consider conservative Rosedale Bible Institute in Ohio for my first college years. He felt that the conservative theological foundations of Rosedale would serve me well. He was concerned that the clash between the Goshen ethos and my Muslim heritage might bewilder me. However, it seemed to me that Goshen would best enable me to acquire the academic credentials I needed to return to Somalia with professional training in areas that the Somali government would respect.

Marcus had keen insight into the challenges of serving in Somalia, and he understood my commitments. Those days on the road with Marcus were extraordinary as we explored many areas of life and faith together. His wise insights imparted on that trip were a further step in my integration of the gospel and life.

Pluralist societies

My different worlds were becoming enormously diverse. The tension between my Bulo Burte roots, where I memorized the Qur'an, and WMHS, where I studied biology, was like a rubber band stretched so taut you could hear it twang. Now I was anticipating Goshen College which would stretch the band even more. In all these transitions the advice of my mother was pertinent. She counseled, "When you travel, if you are hosted by people with only one eye, then become a one-eyed person."

I take a double advice from that proverb. First, I identify with the people among whom I live without a judgmental spirit. If they are different from me, I look at them with only one eye. I do not fixate on their shortcomings but look at them with the good eye that rejoices in the values I can embrace. Second, as my home moves from culture to culture, I need to immerse myself in the culture in which I am present. If they are one-eyed, I need to become one-eyed. This means that I bless and do not curse my hosts no matter how different they might be than my people. Thus, I follow two complementary principles. When it is not against my principles I adopt the local culture; when I choose not to adopt the culture, I try to relate to my host culture with a non-judgmental spirit.

I enrolled at Goshen College, watching whether the faculty and students would be one- or two-eyed human beings. At the same time, I was not a relativist. I knew where I stood, for Christ was the center pole (udub) of my home and the church was my family. I could live with appreciation and flexibility among any people, no matter how different they might be, because I knew where I had come from and I knew where I was going.

Goshen College

Goshen College became a kind of Mecca for Somalis who had been educated in Somalia Mennonite Mission schools, and who were fleeing the atrocities of the Siad Barre regime in Somalia. That fall of 1975, five Somalis enrolled: Mohamed Abdullahi Agane, Salah Warsame, Abdulaziz Shaarif, Hassan Siad Togane, and myself. By the next year, eight Somalis were on campus and for awhile there were thirteen of us. Professor Roy Umble nicknamed us "the Somali Fraternity." We Somalis were rather rambunctious; our laughter and boisterous talk echoed about the campus. We were not inhibited; we were known and obviously present. I became very involved in the international students association and in my senior year I was elected its president.

The highlight of my Goshen College years was involvement in Assembly Mennonite Church. This church was mostly a student movement that had begun only the year before I arrived. This was a fellowship where no questions were off limits. What a dramatic contrast that was to the mosque in Bulo Burte! Yet Assembly was a church clearly centered in Jesus Christ as revealed in the New Testament and in the total biblical witness concerning the Christ. We experienced a quality of fellowship I had never experienced before. These Christians cared for each other; they were a community committed to finding the way together. They formed my theology even more deeply than did the Goshen College experience.

Also important for my Goshen years was my deepening relationship with Eastern Mennonite Missions, whose offices were 500 miles (800 kilometers) east of Goshen in Salunga, Pennsylvania. EMM had placed Mennonites in Somalia as early as 1953. I had occasionally visited with Mennonite missionaries when I was in school in Mogadishu. When the Mennonites had to leave Somalia, beginning in 1972, some of the missionaries were reassigned to the Salunga offices. When these staff people came to Goshen College, they would always meet me and the other Somalis. Especially significant were the faithful contacts that Harold and Barbara Reed and Kenneth and Elizabeth Nissley cultivated.

For school breaks I stayed occasionally in the homes of Ken

and Elizabeth Nissley or Marc and Nancy Erickson. As much as I relished the excellent academic program at Goshen, the most important part of my formation were these deepening relationships with Mennonite church and mission, as well as with significant and enduring friends such as the Nissleys and Ericksons.

As I was wrapping up my final year at Goshen, four events in distant lands disrupted the Islamic and global world order as we had known it. That year, 1979, was a watershed in the Islamic world. First, Russia invaded Afghanistan, with complex long-term implications for relations between Islam and the West. Second, Ayatollah Khomeini returned from exile in Paris to inaugurate the Iranian Islamic Revolution. Third, a Wahhabist insurgency in Arabia occupied the Grand Mosque in Mecca. Fourth, in Somalia the governing Socialist Party was formed. Especially significant was the emergence of militant jihadist Islam as a consequence of these developments. The seeds of contemporary jihadism were being planted in the Middle East and South Central Asia. Within the quiet enclave of Goshen College I never imagined that the events of 1979 would profoundly affect the shape of my ministry in the next decades.

Peace studies at Associated Mennonite Biblical Seminary

In the meantime I graduated from Goshen with a BS in economics. My intention was to go on to graduate school to major in public administration. But a couple of events occurred in my senior year that deflected me from that immediate goal.

I was a close friend of one of the Ethiopian students. We and other students were having dinner in the home of Nancy Hertzler, another student. After dinner we were watching the reports on ABC news of Ethiopian F5 warplanes bombing the town of Jijiga in the Somali-Ethiopia borderlands. It was horrible; the exploding bombs were hurtling body parts and blood everywhere. Nancy wept as she watched with us.

Then Nancy said, "You are good friends. Why are you killing each other?"

I could not forget that question.

Shortly after that, John Howard Yoder, from Associated Mennonite Biblical Seminary (AMBS) and the University of Notre Dame, spoke to the international politics class on campus. He observed, "When I wear a military uniform and kill, it is considered the right thing to do. But when I kill without a uniform it is called murder. Is there any real difference?"

These questions influenced my decision to go to AMBS after graduation to study under John Howard Yoder. Especially transforming were my studies with Yoder and with anthropologist and missiologist Roelf Kuitse and ethicist J. R. Burkholder. Most influential as a mentor and friend was J. R. Burkholder. He attended Assembly Mennonite Church where I also attended during my college and seminary years. He took a keen interest in me, a commitment that endures. He was a spiritual elder for me and profoundly formed my commitments to Christ-centered peacemaking.

My peace theology foundations were profoundly shaped in that incredible year at AMBS (1979–80). After a year at AMBS, I enrolled in graduate school at Indiana State University, Terre Haute, Indiana, where I followed through with my commitment to earn a degree in Public Administration (1980–81). I hoped that with this degree in my pocket the doors would open for me to return to Somalia to serve in the public square—and that is what happened!

Eastbrook Church and Somalia

As I was concluding my studies at Indiana State, Dr. Marc Erickson contacted me. He had a specific proposal and an invitation. "I am inviting you to come to the Eastbrook Church in Milwaukee," he said. "You can serve as an intern in international student ministries for six months. We will pay you a stipend. Then you can return to Somalia, flying with a ticket that the church will purchase for you." I could not imagine a better plan. I was grateful that he wanted me to serve on his team.

Although I had no sponsor for my studies at Goshen and had studied in two graduate schools, I was debt free and thus ready to leave for Somalia. God's provision amazed me! I was given tuition scholarships at Goshen and AMBS, as well as a graduate assistantship at Indiana State. I worked over the summers and participated in work-study programs during the academic year. Marc Erickson also contributed generously. So I graduated from three academic institutions with no debt! I could go to Somalia with no financial obligations.

With delight I accepted Marc's invitation. In January 1982 I joined the Eastbrook Church as an intern in international student ministries. I was to serve until August but I was so eager to return to my homeland that I asked Marc to shorten my internship and he agreed. Eight years before, I had landed at O'Hare Airport in Chicago; now on June 3, 1982, I was boarding a plane at O'Hare for Somalia and East Africa, flying via Rome. So much had happened in the years between my arrival and departure from O'Hare! These eight years had been packed with unanticipated challenge and opportunities.

Martha!

Someone very special remained behind at Eastbrook Church, however. She was jovial Martha Jean Wilson. Her home city was Richmond, Indiana. She had moved to Milwaukee for work and became a member of the Eastbrook Church. During the months of my internship we were drawn into a special friendship. Yet we realized that the cultural leap was enormous—both for Martha, an African American from urban America, and for me, whose roots were Muslim and in small-town Somalia. It's hard to imagine greater diversity brought into a marriage. We entrusted our relationship to the Lord, just as I was entrusting my return to Somalia to the Lord. But I hoped and prayed that our friendship would in God's own time lead to the privilege of serving my people as a husband-wife team.

CHAPTER 5

Serving Within Muslim Society
Somalia
(1982–87)

If you do not see the world, you are blind.
—Somali proverb

IT had been ten years since I as a twenty-year-old had climbed onto the back of a truck in Mogadishu for the two-week trek to Nairobi. During those years I had nurtured a lively engagement with my extensive network of relations and with fellow Somalis, both in North America and in Somalia. Nowadays the mobile phone hugely facilitates that networking, but there were no mobiles or emails in the 1970s, and in Somalia phones were often out of order. Nevertheless, I kept engaged through the vast, largely oral communication network that Somali travelers and the diaspora had developed by the 1980s. So, although returning to my homeland filled me with both trepidation and expectancy, I felt that I would not be an outsider. I knew where I belonged, I had kept in touch, and I had followed the news of my home country.

Called to Somalia
As far as I know none of my Somali friends have returned to live in Somalia after moving abroad to complete their education. Some have returned for prolonged visits, but not to live. One

reason for this has been the political and economic chaos that began in the 1970s and continues even now with no abatement in sight.

However, it was clear to me that God was calling me to invest my life in serving my people. I did not know what lay ahead. I had no plans and no invitation for employment. No agency or person was inviting me. I had no source of support in mind. I just knew that God was calling me to return to my people. So in 1982 I boarded that plane to fly home in obedience.

Somalia was a wounded nation. Siad Barre still ruled the country ruthlessly, and opposition forces threatened the disintegration of his government. The nation was engaged in a brutal war with Ethiopia. There were over a million refugees with 750,000 of them in camps, mostly in Kenya. The economy was a catastrophe. There were several Christian agencies attempting to provide humanitarian assistance. A few months before my return in 1982 a small cadre of Somalia Mennonite Mission teachers had been invited to return. I pondered what my niche might be.

Who am I?

Not only had Somalia undergone radical changes; I too had also been transformed. I had left as a youth whose horizons were largely bounded by a Bulo Burte ethos; I was returning as a man who had been immersed in vastly different contexts. For eight years I had been a student in four academic institutions: Western Mennonite High School, Goshen College, Associated Mennonite Biblical Seminary, and Indiana State University. I had been deep in the powerful and sometimes contradictory cross-currents of American academia.

Now I was going back home. Who had I become? What gift would I offer my people? Those questions pushed me to reflect carefully on the conflicts that were eroding civil society in Somalia. What had I learned in my American experience that could be helpful? Or had I become so different from my people that I would have nothing to offer? Those questions forced me to examine my commitments in a world that struggled with diverse responses to the questions of justice, truth, change, and pluralist societies. Even in Somalia, each clan engaged in the inter-clan wars in Somalia was sure that its cause was just and true. A Somali proverb says: *Ninan dhul marin dhaya maleh* (If you do not see the world you are blind). Ethnocentric societies can become afflicted with that kind of blindness. My father helped me cultivate the gift of seeing the world. He had worked with the Italians and the British, and he moved with ease among the diverse clans of Somali society. But he always did this as the son of Haile Afrahyare. In all my journeys I too never forgot where I had come from. As I was now returning to my people, I had not forgotten who I am.

I grew up in the home of Ali Haile Afrahyare and Hersia Shirar, devoted Muslims and settled nomads in Bulo Burte. However, the last ten years had introduced me to vastly different worlds. To become blind to those worlds would mean that I had become ethnocentric with the likelihood of slipping into xenophobia and rigid conservatism. The death of culture happens when the society insists that it has the best culture; that is the disease which is afflicting the Somali culture today. The radical al-Shabab movement is seeking to impose a rigid Islam on Somalia. These youthful revolutionaries believe not only that they are the best, but also that all alternatives should be destroyed.

My eyes first began to open to new worlds in 1968 when an Australian Christian nurse nurtured me back to health after my near death from a cerebral malaria attack. That was the first time I had met a Christian. Two years later I was occasionally in the home of Marc and Nancy Erickson when the whole international missionary team was present. Several years in the May 15 High School revealed a world beyond Mogadishu. The rambunctious debates we had with the Marxist and atheistic Russian teachers enlarged my horizons.

On my fourteen-day trek from Mogadishu to Nairobi by truck through acacia scrublands I shall never forget traversing the Turkana tribal areas; I was astounded to see women walking along the road with only a loin cloth, breasts fully exposed. For the eyes of a conservative twenty-year-old this was a tremendous shock. In Nairobi even the church scene was hugely diverse: the Nairobi Pentecostal Church, the Somali Fellowship, or the Mennonite Church. In Islam all worship is the same throughout the world. In Nairobi I met Christian diversity.

My eight years in American academia also immersed me in enormous diversity, not only in regard to people, values, and beliefs, but also within the world of ideas. How does one find a center within the cacophonies of an Enlightenment worldview, biblical theism, New Ageism, relativism, agnosticism, scientism, individualism, religious pluralism, materialism, secular humanism, social activism, and evangelical Christianity? The collision of the Marxism and Islam of my youth seemed a distant echo in the dissonant themes of the American context. Some of my peers became lost as they struggled through the cacophony. While many have contributed marvelously to community uplift, others have lost faith in God or have succumbed to alcohol and the lure of American materialism. To use the words of the Nigerian writer, Chinua Achebe, for them, "things fall apart."[1]

The church and culture change

My life also would have fallen apart if it were not for the church. Writing from a Nigerian perspective, Achebe sees the church as irrelevant and even counter to the wholesome functioning of traditional tribal society. In contrast, I have experienced the church as my primary integrative community. Ever since that day in Marc Erickson's home in 1970 when I committed my life to Christ, I have known not only where I have come from, but also where I am going. The direction of my journey is my home in Christ, and the church is the community of reconciliation that Christ is creating. I have never been a Christian alone. Ever since my conversion, I have always been committed to the fellowship of the church.

The church in all its variety exists within the diversity of local and global cultures; those cultures are sometimes in conflict. In Somalia today there is conflict between clans. Conflict can be destructive, but it is not always destructive. The philosopher Hegel got it right when he observed that it is in conflict that progress emerges. As my Marxist high school teachers explained it, every synthesis of conflicting cultures provides opportunity for a new thesis or ideal.

I saw that process unfolding within my own Somali family and within the mosque in my community. My mother was illiterate. I learned the Qur'an and taught her some key verses. As she memorized these verses, our home began to change with greater emphasis on being good Muslims. Then I learned the right way to pray and taught it to my mother. So she began to pray in the right way. The next ideal was Islamic law, and again our home began to change in the direction of living according to Muslim law. This is the normal direction in all Islamic societies; the longer a society is Muslim the more that society converges with the norms established in Islamic systems of law. The process is gradual, beginning with the confession of faith that there is no God but Allah and that Muhammad is the prophet of Allah. Islamic law is not on the cultural horizon when the confession of faith is first made. However, as the Islamization of the society progresses, new Islamic ideals are acknowledged step by step.

The small Christian witness in Bulo Burte, comprised of an international missionary team, was also an agent of change. The presence of the little hospital became a beacon of hope as it modeled modest but excellent medical care. The force inspiring the hospital was not Hegel's evolving philosophical ideal, but rather Jesus Christ. The hospital showed how the church is a community whose goal is the fulfillment of the kingdom of God as revealed in Jesus. He is the ideal toward which God is calling all of history. Redemptive compassionate love is at the center, and is always in tension with the norms of prevailing cultures. Yet as the church both incarnates and is influenced by that vision, the church becomes a community of life-giving change within culture.

John Paul Lederach, an authority on conflict transformation, has helped me see that a dimension of the mission of the church is its calling to conflict transformation.[2] He does not push for conflict eradication, but rather works at transforming conflict into constructive alternatives. I believe that the vision for conflict transformation is one way that the church can be a life-giving community.

Lederach leans heavily upon the insights and tools of sociology in his approach to conflict transformation, and I have found those insights helpful in my own work in peacemaking. I also explore the resources for peacemaking within my traditional Somali culture as well as within Islam. However, I believe that ultimately it is Christ who is the Healer and the authentic Reconciler. Our human condition alone is insufficient for authentic reconciliation. We need Jesus; we need the grace and forgiveness he offers in the cross and resurrection; we need the Holy Spirit.

What gift could I offer?

If it were not for my Christ-centered approach to cultural diversity, conflict, and change, I would become a relativist floundering among the callings of the multiple cultures in which I have lived. I am a cultural relativist with a center. As my mother counseled, if the people have only one eye, become one-eyed. That counsel has some similarities with the decision of the early church as recorded in Acts 15 at the momentous Jerusalem Conference. At that meeting the church decided that Gentiles would remain within their culture and Jews within theirs, but that each were called to a Christ-centered faith expressing the righteousness of Christ within their cultural context. This was a vision of a Christ-centered cultural relativism. As the church grew within Gentile areas, the cultural implications of the Jerusalem Conference developed in astonishing ways. Gentiles could eat pork but needed to abstain from fornication. Jews could be circumcised but were encouraged to eat freely with Gentiles whom they had previously spurned. The Jerusalem Conference determined that a Christ-centered approach to cultural and religious pluralism would relativize culture, while also holding to Christ as the firm and universal center.

I knew that I was returning to a Somalia plagued by a toxic culture of intensifying violence. Things were literally falling apart. Similarly, Nigerian culture was in stress when Chinua Achebe wrote his novel, *Things Fall Apart*, in 1958. The stressors that he discerned between modernizing forces and traditionalist values are also relevant to the Somali experience. In

Somalia, Christian missions such as the Somalia Mennonite Mission were viewed as modernizing influences, especially through the schools. The society was divided by modernizing themes and the traditionalist nomadic ethos. I knew that my presence in Somalia would be identified as a modernizing voice. Yet in my soul I knew that neither the modernizing nor traditionalist forces held the key for the healing of our society.

Achebe drew some of his insights from a provocative little poem by William Butler Yeats entitled "The Second Coming," written during the horrendous destruction of World War I. In his dark assessment of the war, Yeats writes of innocence gone and anarchy prevailing: "Things fall apart; the center cannot hold." Although Yeats struggled with faith, in the midst of the maelstrom of war he alludes to the hope born in Bethlehem.

That brief poem grips me as it did Achebe. It so powerfully describes the Somalia to which I was returning. I knew I was returning to a society that was falling apart, where the center was not holding. Only twenty-two years earlier Somalia had become an independent, modern nation-state with a boisterous parliamentary democracy and exuberant hope. All of that had unraveled and the hopes born a generation ago were shattered.

How would all of this work out as I returned to Somalia? As I began my journey back, I reaffirmed that same Bethlehem hope. It is an unobtrusive hope centered in the One born in a manger, on the edges of power, a hope born within conflict. The children of Bethlehem were killed shortly after the birth of Mary's child. Yet he is the presence of peace among us. He is the presence of God among us. I knew that my return to Somalia was Christ's appointment for me. The gift I was bringing was to be an emissary of Jesus, the One who is the Bethlehem hope.

Finding my niche

On my way back to Africa, I stopped in Rome for a week to network with the Somali community, friends, and relatives. That was a helpful orientation to what I could anticipate in Somalia. Then on June 10, 1982, I arrived in Mogadishu. As I stepped onto the tarmac, I was refreshed with the salty ocean breezes wending inland from the Indian Ocean. The noisy chaos in the crowded immigration and customs area invigorated me. I saw my brother Mohammed and we shouted greetings above the bedlam. Finally I was through customs and was being embraced by friends and family. My heart overflowed with joy. We feasted that night and talked non-stop, often at the same time. A day later, Mohammed and I traveled to Bulo Burte. Father killed a goat; Mother cooked it in just the right way with my favorite seasoning, and we enjoyed a bounteous feast.

The first Friday that I was back in Mogadishu, I worshipped with the Somali Believers Fellowship—or, as the wider society referred to it, the People of the Messiah. The believers avoided the term *Christian* because in the Somali context it included connotations of alcohol abuse and loose living. Somalis got this notion from observing the lifestyle of many of the former Western colonial occupiers who attended church on Sundays but whose way of living contradicted conservative Muslim sensitivities. *Christian* was considered a synonym to *Western*, which did not enjoy good press among Muslim Somalis.

A New Testament conversation reminds us that disciples of Jesus sometimes also struggled with a bad press. Philip, an observer of Jesus, found his friend Nathaniel and invited him to come and see the one whom the prophets wrote about. Philip asserted that the promised Savior had appeared—Jesus of Nazareth.

Nathaniel responded sarcastically, "Nazareth! Can anything good come from there?"

Philip refused to be sidelined. "Come and see!" he implored (John 1:43-46).

Similarly, a skeptical attitude prevails across much of the Muslim world, where the settled assumption is that nothing good can come from the West. So if the Christian faith is Western, it has to be defective and objectionable. Even any sign reminding people of the cross is objectionable, because the cross conjures memories of the Crusaders who a thousand years ago killed Muslims under the sign of the cross.

So we Somali believers usually avoided calling ourselves Christians. Nevertheless, I knew that I could not evade questions of religious identity. The Somali people are thoroughly religious and have no respect for irreligious people. Finding my niche within the faith community in Somalia, therefore, would be vital to my effectiveness as a development expert. Who I am was more important than my expertise. I needed to be clearly understood not as a flag waving ideologue, but as a person who knew his spiritual home. So on my first Friday in Mogadishu, I worshipped with the Somali Believers Fellowship. In doing so, I had quietly made a clear statement in regard to my faith identity. The fellowship met in a small room in the Catholic Cathedral at the center of the city. The bishop was supportive of this small Protestant fellowship of about twenty people.

Prior to the nationalization of the Somalia Mennonite Mission in 1972, Somalis in Mogadishu who had come to faith in Christ met for weekly worship on the SMM premises, and as long at the SIM was present, some also met at the SIM premises. After nationalization that was not possible. So the Somali Believers Fellowship met in the Cathedral. Somali believers continued to meet after the SIM and SMM left Somalia. They met on Friday, because in Muslim Somalia Friday was the official day of rest, whereas Sunday was a regular work day. In addition to Somali believers, there were a few expatriates, including several Eastern Mennonite Missions teachers and my friends, Kenneth and Elizabeth Nissley, who directed the EMM program in Somalia. Although the Somali Mennonite Mission was dissolved after nationalization and all missionaries were requested to leave in 1976, by 1982 there was a small group who were invited to return to work in university level education.

At church that first Friday, I met Art DeFehr. He and his wife, Leona, were Mennonite Brethren from Winnipeg, Canada. He was serving as ambassador of the United Nations High Commission for Refugees (UNHCR) in Somalia. He felt that with my education in political science and economics I should consider working in the political arena, and urged me to write a resume. Interestingly, President Siad Barre had already offered me any job I wanted within the government. I resisted going in a political administrative direction, however, for political systems inherently tend to divide. I wanted to work in ministries of reconciliation and humanitarian aid.

I did write my resume, and within days World Vision invited me to become the director of relief and development operations for their expanding program in Somalia. I accepted that invitation. In addition, a variety of agencies serving in Somalia sought my counsel, so I was pulled into a widening network whereby I could exert influence on program directions. I was grateful that doors opened for a variety of consultations for humanitarian programs.

The World Vision responsibilities took me to Nairobi for three months to learn their leadership ethos. It was good to be back in Kenya, reconnecting with some of the people I had known during my stay in Nairobi a decade earlier. However, the Africa director of World Vision inadvertently became embroiled in a tendentious political upheaval in West Africa. The reputation of World Vision in Africa was temporarily tarnished, and consequently the World Vision program in Somalia closed.

So by April 1983 my short-lived role with Somali World Vision came to an end. This reinforced my decision to keep distance between my ministry commitments and the political arena; the church is the church and the state is the state. Remarkably, as the World Vision staff left Somalia, they were boarding the same plane that had just brought a new team from the Eastbrook Church. That congregation considered me to be part of their team, and before long they appointed me director of their Somalia development program. I did not miss a beat as far as employment was concerned!

Sometimes I was involved in some strange enterprises. For example, Mennonite Central Committee (MCC)—a relief and development agency of the Mennonite churches—got the notion that crossbreeding camels from Asia with camels from Somalia might produce a more resilient camel. So they asked me to help make this happen. So I explained to my father that it was the Mennonites who provided some of my schooling in America, and that now they needed a bull camel. He was quite enthusiastic about offering them a bull from his herd as a gift. In fact, later he sold another five camels to the MCC breeding project. I made arrangements for herding these camels the five hundred miles from Bulo Burte to Mandera on the remote Kenya–Ethiopia border, where the breeding experiment was to take place. My life had not been routine! A year before, I was studying Adam Smith's theory of capitalism in graduate school at Indiana State University. Now I was organizing a three-week trek through the Somali acacia scrublands for half a dozen breeding camels, hoping that this effort would improve the camel capital of the region. I had hired camel-herders; yet for some days I worked with the herders to make sure the camels got to the right rendezvous.

Those days with the camels in the Somali bush were good for pause and reflection. I was pleased seeing the night sky with no pollution. In the west, I saw one intriguing cluster of stars called the Pleiades; in Somalia the cluster is called "Flock of Goats." After years of living in urban jungles, I was grateful for this brief immersion within with my people's nomadic heritage.

Eastbrook Development Program

By 1983 the Sudan Interior Mission was ready to re-engage in Somalia. Eastbrook Church and its pastor, Marc Erickson, were the visionary powerhouse for the project, although others were also committed. When the team arrived, their first commitment was to reopen the Bulo Burte hospital, which had closed when the SIM withdrew from Somalia in 1974. Marc believed that I should be the director of the SIM program and leader of the team. However, the SIM international leadership did not think it wise to appoint a Somali to administer the Somalia program. When the two different approaches to leadership could not be reconciled, SIM withdrew from Somalia and determined to continue to give special attention to Somali ministries in Kenya. I never understood why the SIM international leadership took their position. However, I determined not to let this decision affect my spirit or attitudes toward the SIM who led me to faith in Christ.

In the end, Eastbrook Church entered Somalia as an independent development agency with a contract with the Ministry of Health to serve the people of Bulo Berte. We registered with the government as Eastbrook Development Program and I was appointed leader of the Eastbrook team. I was committed to the Somali fellowship of believers as well as to the Eastbrook program.

Relating to the church

The Somali Believers Fellowship in Mogadishu comprised about two dozen believers and experienced some growth. At Bulo Burte there were about half a dozen believers. We in the Eastbrook Development Program team tried to encourage the Somali believers, as did SMM. For the Mogadishu fellowship, we gave special attention to leadership training. We tried to help enterprising believers get involved in small business enterprises so that they and the congregations could become self-sufficient. We sought to serve the whole society in ways that contributed to economic support. We collaborated with SMM and Mennonite Central Committee (MCC), who were also developing creative engagement in a variety of programs such as agricultural development, teaching, curriculum development, and, in due course, peacemaking.

The People of God course for Muslims—that we had developed in Eastleigh, Nairobi, fifteen years earlier—was the main tool that we used in Bible studies. There were occasional baptisms, including six university students. We were encouraged in so many ways!

A program with integrity and compassion

As director of the Eastbrook Somali Development Program, I determined that we would commit to a medical program that could be replicated anywhere in Somalia. That meant excellence, modest investment, and self-sustainability. The dependency syndrome that permeated the hospital at Bulo Burte had to be broken. We accomplished this by initiating patient fees. By 1985 the hospital was fully self-sustaining with the exception of the international staff.

The Bulo Burte medical program caught the attention of the government, whose hospitals were chronically underfunded and consequently short-staffed, without adequate drugs. A government delegation visited our hospital. They were impressed and determined that our hospital would be the model for all hospitals in Somalia. This was an example of the role of the church in bringing transformation into a culture.

Our total program had a budget of $150 thousand, whereas the Italian Aid mission up river in Beled Weyne had a budget of $14 million per year. Yet they had almost no influence on the society or the culture. The Italian development team stayed within their staff compounds. The young people on our team intermingled with the townspeople and they were greatly loved. Jesus said that we are the light and the salt of the world (Matthew 5:13-16). The light from Bulo Burte was gently penetrating the local community as well as the medical programs throughout.

We invested in a variety of programs. The leaders of the Mogadishu fellowship gave attention to the educational aspirations of young people. One very successful enterprise I initiated as a self-help program was the digging of a well in Ceelbuur 120 miles (193 kilometers) north of Bulo Burte. The well is still producing water to this day. Such programs were in direct response to the needs and requests of the people among whom we served. The townspeople valued our work and our desire to share our lives with them.

We functioned with utmost integrity; we never gave a bribe. If an officer demanded money, we would say, "Let's go to the police station and report to them what you are demanding." Likewise, we were impeccable in our financial reporting. All our imports for our programs were carefully documented and reported. We paid our taxes in full without fudging on anything. Eastbrook earned a reputation for integrity that was fundamental to our commitment to being faithful ambassadors for Christ.

Marriage to Martha

As the Eastbrook program developed, a wonderful gift was the arrival of Martha as a short-term missionary on the Eastbrook team. She came to be closer to where I was serving, as well as to learn about my people. She developed a love and commitment to them. For Martha to be part of the team was a gift of God's grace. As she served with me, she was challenged by the ministry and by God's calling on her life. What would be involved if we were to partner as husband and wife to share Christ among the Somalis?

Toward the end of her two-year term we stopped seeing one another and committed our relationship to prayer. I returned to the United States for a year sabbatical. Martha returned to the United States after her term was completed. Then we were drawn back together by our love for one another and our desire to live a great adventure with God together. So after much prayer and counseling we were wed on a beautiful autumn day, October 17, 1987, with our pastor Dr. Marc Erickson officiating. Our wedding took place in a beautiful old church on the east side of Milwaukee.

As we have continued together in our ministry, Martha has supported me in the ministries to which God had called me and equipped me. We are a team. We each bring unique gifts into the ministry. We continue to learn what marriage is and how to love each other better.

After our wedding we returned to Somalia together. I had been away for a year, and upon return I was involved with various agencies, giving counsel and encouragement. This included the Somalia Mennonite Mission, but my primary employment was still with Eastbrook. It was at that time that I became increasingly involved in peacemaking efforts. That was a dramatic challenge, as I will describe in the next two chapters.

CHAPTER 6

Struggle for Inclusion
The Muslim Community
(1988)

There is no compulsion in religion.
—Qur'an

WHEN we returned to Somalia, we faced enormous challenges, in the form of opposition to me and to the ministries in which I was involved. There had always been challenges, but the intensity of the opposition now increased. Somali clan and religious leaders were polarized as to how to cope with my presence within the Muslim-Somali ethos. The impasse seemed unresolvable.

Confronting threats

We lived in Mogadishu at the Eastbrook national office, located near the Ministry of Higher Education. We wanted to have meetings with clan leaders, but they refused to come into our home, even for a cup of tea. They believed that those who have left their commitment to Islam must be totally excluded from community life.

There were two matters that gave my opponents special concern. First, they suspected that the successful well-digging in the Ceelbuur area included efforts to make proselytes for the Christian faith. The second concern related to my teaching economics and economic development at the Technical Teachers Training College of the National University. My courses on economics were a hit. Occasionally we invited students to our home. On one occasion forty students from the Lafole College of Education came to our home. Another time seventy from the Gaahiir Faculty of the National University came. Martha's food was delicious and always appreciated by the students. So I was accused of making proselytes not only with the villagers of Ceelbuur, but also of the university students. It was true that several students had become believers in *Issa* (Jesus).

The charges were serious, and four leaders of my clan explicitly threatened to kill me. I knew that my effectiveness would be totally undermined if such an attitude prevailed. I insisted that I was as much a Somali as any of them. I insisted that I seek to honor God in all I do. I reminded them of how much good I had done for them and their families. I told them that I had never made a Christian out of anyone; that is the work of God. I told them that no one has ever gotten any money from any of us as an encouragement to convert.

Two separate watershed events occurred while I sought to remain included in my larger extended family. The first followed the digging of the Ceelbuur well. Some clan leaders saw its success as my attempt to convert local people to my faith. Word of their death threats reached one of my relatives and he insisted we sit down together and address their concerns. So, one afternoon, four religious leaders from the Ceelbuur district came to my house in Mogadishu and met with my nephew, two of my brothers, and myself.

We sat on the veranda and Martha served us cakes and Somali tea. They shared their concerns. I insisted that I was as much a part of the clan as any of them! I stressed that I was seeking to help the community by helping to provide a well for the district. And though I am a believer of Issa, I do not change people. Only God can change human hearts. They received my explanation and were content with it.

The second event was when I was allowed to fully participate in a major family decision regarding a death that had occurred. A young man from another clan had been killed by a man from my clan. The "king" or *ugas* of my clan convened a meeting of all the major family leaders to resolve the situation. The discussions were about reconciliation, restitution, and the payment of compensation to the aggrieved (known as blood wealth). I offered our home as a venue for the meeting. Even though the ugas was in favor, some of the leaders initially refused to attend after my home had been announced as the venue. They said that the plates and spoons in my home were contaminated because I was an apostate. But when the ugas and others entered through my gate these leaders realized the meeting would go forward. While we were meeting, four men came to the gate of our home and demanded that I go out to meet them. Several of my brothers were there in our home, along with leaders from my mother's clan. Together they refused to let me go to the gate and offered to go instead. They found that one of the four was an imam who had openly declared that I must die. Finally, however, the four men consented to come into our home and joined in the meal.

That evening was a defining moment. The symbolic significance of eating together in my home was tremendous; it meant from then on that I was accepted within my clan system and, by extension, within the entire Somali system. I was again an insider. However, being included involves much more than just a meal together. Relationships had to be cultivated. We did that. Every week ten to twenty elders from my clan would come to our home for discussions and food. Martha oversaw the cooking. We ate and fellowshipped and conversed vigorously together. In that way our covenant of peace was renewed each week.

Incarnational witness for Christ

My commitments as an insider were both to the church and to the Somali Muslim community. For me, these commitments were grounded in my convictions about the Christian belief in incarnation. Christians believe that in Jesus the Word has become human. Muslims refer to Jesus as the word. The Qur'an proclaims he is *Issa Kalimatullah*—Jesus the Word of God.[1] This is immensely significant in peacemaking. If Jesus is the Word incarnate, his disciples are called by God to reflect the incarnational presence of Christ.

I was called to seek inclusion not only within the church, but also within the Somali/Muslim community in Mogadishu. The whole city knew that I was a committed believer in Jesus the Messiah and fully engaged as an insider within the church. They also knew that I had become accepted as an insider within the Somali/Muslim community. As a member of the church, I sought to be a sign of the incarnation within the Somali/Muslim community. The breakthrough happened when the Somali leaders ate in my home. They had accepted my presence as a disciple of Jesus within their community.

Some feel that in order to be accepted as an insider, believers in the Messiah must mute their witness. I disagree. The notion of hiding our witness reminds me of Bilal, the first black Muslim believer in Islam. When in Mecca Muhammad appointed Bilal to give the prayer call five times daily. However, Bilal was afraid of the Meccans so when he gave the prayer call, he would mutter the call into a clay pot. So the call was muted. No one heard it. And the Muslim movement did not grow.

Then Muhammad and the Muslims migrated to Medina, where the message of Islam was more openly welcomed than in Mecca. In Medina, Bilal could give the prayer call without fear. So he proclaimed the call from the minaret for all to hear. Consequently the movement grew. Likewise, believers in Jesus the Messiah need to find ways to express their witness from the minaret, as it were. I have tried to express my witness to Christ from a variety of metaphorical minarets.

Identification with the church

My regular attendance at church was observed by the whole Muslim community in Mogadishu. I not only attended, but I was also an active participant and occasionally served on the council of elders. Three times I was arrested for my involvement in the church. One evening officers came to the home of Kenneth and Elizabeth Nissley when I was participating in an elders' meeting. They called for me from the gate, and when I stepped outside they whisked me off to jail.

No one in the meeting knew what had happened; all they knew is that I did not return to the meeting. So they launched a search, going from police station to police station, as well as to the jails. All officers asserted that they knew nothing about me. Late into the evening they found the jail where I was being held. The next morning I was released. I did not let this kind of intimidation dissuade me from full engagement in the life and ministry of the church. That commitment was one form of minaret for Christ.

On another occasion my minaret was bearing witness in court when there was an attempted rape of a female MCC worker. The assailant was taken to court and I was called to serve as language interpreter in the case—the Nissleys were also there. This was a high profile court case in the National Security Court. The judge ordered me to swear by the Qur'an that I would tell the truth. I responded, "I am a follower of Jesus the Messiah, and therefore I will not swear."

In unison, the whole courtroom gasped, "Ooooooooooooooo!"

The judge persisted, "Will you tell the truth?"

I responded, "Absolutely!"

Then the judge invited me to proceed with my work as interpreter.

That courtroom was my minaret. Through the grapevine many heard my word of witness and confession of faith that day. That kind of boldness has not shut the door on inclusion for me. Of course, I have needed to persist, sometimes even demanding inclusion. In my journey I have found that vigilant persistence is important.

Transition and upheaval

When I was away on sabbatical, 1986–87, an expatriate carried the leadership of the Eastbrook program. When Martha and I returned to Mogadishu after our marriage, Somalia was already being transformed by forces of destruction. As the decade of the 1980s progressed, the nation lurched in tragic directions.

We grieved that our return had to be cut short. The war with Ethiopia ran out of steam with huge losses on both sides. Civil war engulfed the northern regions and soon spilled south toward Mogadishu. The inter-clan conflicts were not abating, and forces opposing President Siad Barre were gaining momentum.

With medical services deteriorating, Martha left in July 1988, a couple of months before our first baby was due. I left a month later, in August. We left with the intention of returning to Somalia after the birth of our first child, but that became impossible and we decided to stay in the United States. The rest of the Eastbrook team remained for another year. Yet tensions were building, especially in Mogadishu. The Eastbrook office moved to a location near a mosque, where all the comings and goings at the center were easily observed. Eastbrook's logo was the sign of the dove and the cross and it was imprinted on our vehicles. Some felt that this explicitly Christian logo was needlessly offensive. However, I do not believe these logos had anything to do with the developing conflict. The tensions that year were to be part of a wider pattern of inter-clan strife.

On July 9, 1989, the beloved Catholic bishop, Father Salvadoro Columbo, was killed in Mogadishu. By July 14 areas of the city were engulfed in rioting, and the Eastbrook office in Mogadishu was destroyed. Ironically, at that time Marc Erickson and I were in Manila attending Lausanne II, a global conference on carrying forward to all nations the good news of salvation in Christ. We only heard about the destruction after our team had safely evacuated.

The attack was planned so that three groups in turn would ransack the modest Eastbrook center. The mobs declared their intention to kill the missionaries. Darryl and Debbie Zeibarth and their three young children hid in a room with a large glass door. The three ransacking teams trashed every room in the center, but did not touch that glass door. We believe the angels of God were stationed at the door. When the gangs had gone, the Zeibarths slipped away to an adjoining house, but hid each of their children in barrels in the yard.

The same day a similar scenario was poised for explosion in Bulo Burte. The mosque preacher delivered a vitriolic sermon denouncing the Eastbrook team and calling for an attack. However, the town fathers arrested the preacher and imprisoned him. The town authorities put a cordon around the Eastbrook hospital and residences. That night Muslims from the town slept in the yard around the homes of the missionaries as a human shield of protection. The next day these brave Muslim defenders of their Christian guests escorted the Eastbrook team to Mogadishu for safe evacuation. No one was hurt; no one killed.

When the evacuation from the Mogadishu city center to the airport commenced, it was those very persons who had at one time hesitated to eat with us and who had threatened my life who escorted the Eastbrook team safely out of the city to the airport. They did this at considerable risk to their lives. The imam himself, who had spearheaded those first death threats, rode in the front seat, the most vulnerable spot in the escape vehicle!

I felt that my persistence in the struggle for inclusion had been vindicated. Had I been content to be pushed into the outsider role, I do not believe these men would have escorted the team to safety. But when the walls of exclusion were breached, the open doors for inclusion were not only extended to me, but also to all members of our team. And in all of this I want to stress the ministry of prayer. Both in Somalia and in lands afar, servants of the Lord fell on their knees in prayer. God responded in ways that can only be described as miraculous. God was graciously caring for his servants.

We grieved the destruction, violence, and death in Somalia. However, as the events unfolded, it was clear that our decision to stay in the United States had been correct. We were committed to following the counsel of the Holy Spirit and of our brothers and sisters who affirmed our decision. The fate of the Catholic bishop could well have become my fate as well, as destructive violence spread across Somalia.

Just over two years after we returned to the United States, on January 26, 1991, Siad Barre fled the country. His ruinous twenty-two-year experiment with Marxist-Leninist political theory was dead. In the years that followed, the Somali people floundered from crisis to crisis as they sought to find healing for their wounded nation.

Suffering for Christ

We thank God for the many signs of his protecting presence in Somalia. However, we also recognize that not all Somali disciples of Jesus were rescued from death; in the turmoil, a number were killed. By 1994 most believers had died or fled the country. For some, God's miraculous intervention awaits the final resurrection when Christ returns. The circumstances of their deaths were varied. One brother knew that his life was under threat, but decided to stay. He had a vision of a barrel of sweet honey suspended in the sky above Somalia and then emptied across the land bringing new life wherever the honey flowed. He believed this barrel was Christ and the honey the Holy Spirit whom Christ would pour out across the wounded peoples of Somalia. He stayed to be a channel through whom this new life would flow. Shortly after this vision he was killed, leaving a widow and a young child.

These martyrs who were faithful disciples are now in heaven as part of that great cloud of witnesses cheering us on in the faith (Hebrews 12:1).

Afrahyare!

As events were unfolding in Somalia, we were back in Milwaukee. On September 17, 1988, we were blessed with the birth of our firstborn son, Afrahyare! We named him after his renowned great-grandfather.

This name was bestowed on our son in Somalia when he was still in Martha's womb. Just before she left Somalia for the birth of our baby, the paramount chief (ugas) of my clan came to our home with clan elders to give her a gift as well as a blessing. The ugas said that Martha would bear a son, and that his name would be Afrahyare, the name of my grandfather. He had been a highly respected confidant of the ugas.

As I held Afrah I prayed for an anointing of wisdom to discern what the next steps might be for us in our calling to serve the Somali people. Within my soul there was the deepening conviction that Christ was leading me into a ministry of peacemaking. Afrahyare was a sign of that calling, for his name was bequeathed by the ugas who had warmly included me in the clan family, knowing that I was a follower of Jesus. I believed that Christ was calling me to be an ambassador of the gospel of peace.

CHAPTER 7

Wounded Peacemaker
Immersion in the Somali Conflict
(1989–92)

Give your enemy fresh milk.
—Somali Proverb

THE reprieve in the United States was an unexpected interruption for Martha and me. I had been in Somalia most of the past six years and Martha most of the last three. We had planned to return to Somalia as soon as our baby son was ready to travel and assumed our stay in the United States would be short. EMM was increasing their personnel in Somalia. After the attack on the Development Program offices, however, Eastbrook had no one serving in Somalia. Eastbrook decided to wait and see what developed. One family remained in Nairobi, Kenya, hoping the violence would abate so that they could return. As for us, we had no peace about returning. We believed that the same forces that had killed the Catholic bishop would target us if we returned.

Equipping for peacemaking

Finally we made the difficult decision to postpone our return to Somalia. We left Milwaukee and dear friends at the Eastbrook Church and moved to Elkhart, Indiana, to pursue more intentional peace studies at Associated Mennonite Biblical Seminary (AMBS)—where I had studied for a year following my graduation from Goshen College. I believed that peacemaking was the new and urgent frontier for Christian engagement in Somalia. To further equip me for that commitment, I needed more theological and practical training, and AMBS had a strong academic program in peace studies.

We were sometimes overwhelmed with the challenges of caring for our baby, Afrah—much as we enjoyed him!—and with an exceedingly tight budget and hard-hitting academics as our studies commenced at AMBS. A further concern was deep tension within our marriage. Cross-cultural marriages always create special challenges. I brought my Somali perspectives on marriage, and Martha brought her North American ones. These different views were complementary and enriching, but we did not always see it that way.

My father was my role model, and her mother was her role model. My father was an ideal Somali husband, but that role model clashed with the values from Martha's home. A healthy marriage is like two people holding opposite ends of a thread. When one person pulls, the other must yield, or the thread will break. We were not yielding the thread adequately. Consequently our marriage was in distress, and so we often sought counsel from others. How we thank God that our marriage was preserved! After the formidable pressures in Somalia, AMBS was a good place to work on building a strong marriage.

At the same time, we worked on our academic programs. I completed my degree in peace studies and Martha focused on theological studies with an emphasis on church history. Martha worked in the bookstore and I worked as custodian. I also worked in the library, and for a time I served in student development at nearby Goshen College.

This was a blessed time for renewing our fellowship with the Assembly Church in nearby Goshen that had meant so much to me during my college days. Martha learned much about Mennonites and Anabaptists during this time. We were in Elkhart for most of our nearly six-year stay in the United States—from Afrah's first Christmas in 1988 until July 1994, with only three periods of absence for trips to Somalia and Stockholm.

My parents

Martha and I were immersed in the challenges of academia when, on January 15, 1990, my father died. As much as we enjoyed the libraries at AMBS, I believe I absorbed more of genuine value from my father and mother (who was to die thirteen years later in 2003) than in the many books that I have read. Unknown to them, in quiet ways their spiritual insights and practices were used by the Holy Spirit to plant within my soul a spiritual quest that Jesus has now fulfilled. I often felt that in the many ways that they blessed me and supported my decision to believe in Christ, they blessed not only me, but also the Christ who is the center of my life.

Furthermore, my later involvement with clan leaders in nonviolent peacemaking was significantly formed by the quest for peace that my father practiced. The traditional, pre-Islamic approaches to peacemaking that I will describe shortly are based upon my father's example and teaching. However, the Christian gospel takes us beyond the possibilities within the traditional system, especially in regard to forgiveness, even of the enemy.

Working with Ergo (peace envoys)

During the troubles leading to the exile of President Siad Barre, the Somali diaspora was working with MCC, the Quakers, and the Life and Peace Institute in Sweden in forming a peacemaking fraternity to address the challenges of Somalia. The first meeting convened December 14, 1990, in Harrisonburg, Virginia, at Eastern Mennonite College (now called Eastern Mennonite University). They were known as Ergo, or in Somali, *Ergada* (envoys for peace). John Paul Lederach was a key non-Somali player. The visionaries included quite a number of the Somali diaspora who were scholars, including myself. Some had been influenced by SMM schools decades earlier.

On January 26, 1991, only six weeks after the inception of Ergo, the Barre regime was overthrown. The inter-clan strife related to the upheaval in Somalia projected right into the diaspora communities. So the first challenge was to work toward peace among the disparate clans within the diaspora. That commitment absorbed much of the energy of the group for the first months after its creation.

Various delegations to Somalia boldly challenged the belligerents to seek a day when the young boys would learn to read rather than learning to use guns. Early in 1991 my family and friends in Somalia urged me, too, to come to Somalia to work toward peacemaking. For many generations my family in Somalia had carried a special burden and interest in peacemaking—hence the invitation. So I went with the blessing of Ergo and funding from my family and friends. I was in Somalia for three months.

Others from the Ergo team came to Somalia from time to time to encourage the peace process. One of these peace envoys was the poet Mohamud Siad Togane. When his plane landed, there was a volley of gunfire from different factions near the aircraft. I had come to the airport to receive Togane, and I ducked behind bushes for cover. Alas, Togane thought the gun fire was to honor his arrival. He strode down the steps from the plane totally oblivious to the danger. I shouted mightily, "Duck, duck, duck or you will be killed!" He finally caught on to the dangerous situation and took cover with me in the bushes. He was of a clan that was in rivalry with my clan. But we forgot all of that as we went together to where I was staying and worked together in our inter-clan peacemaking efforts.

Peacemaking in the Somali context

In my role as an advocate for nonviolence, I recognized that there were three levels of peacemaking in which Somalis participated: first, the modern penal system with courts and laws that the colonial authorities had established; second, the Islamic *khadi* court system formed by the Islamic Sharia systems of law; and third, the pre-Islamic systems of justice known as *xeer*. This is justice grounded in covenantal relations and responsibilities. Prior to the collapse of political order, all three of these systems functioned complementarily and in relative harmony. An aggrieved person could choose his system of law and justice.

As the country unraveled in civil unrest and inter-clan conflict, some persuasive voices called for a strengthening of the Islamic system of justice. A core attraction was that Islam invited participation in a community and systems of justice that transcended clan. The Muslim community (ummah) was universal and included all clans. Sharia law was seen to be transcendent, given by God and interpreted by the theologians. The ummah's authority was the Qur'an, which also transcended local clan loyalties. The imams in their sermons hammered away at these themes. They proclaimed Islam as the religion of peace and Muslims as a people of peace who comprised all the clans of Somalia.

In reality, however, the Islamic system as practiced in Somalia has been largely ineffective in peacemaking. A key reason for this is that in Islam justice is disposed toward retributive justice. While Islam can affirm restorative justice, the practice of militant wings of Muslim leadership in Somalia inclined in the direction of retribution. Consequently, as inter-clan conflict developed, the principles of Islamic retribution increased their grip on the clan systems. Retribution deepened the grievances rather than healing broken relations.

Traditional pre-Islamic peacemaking

For this reason leaders engaged in peacemaking began to turn to pre-Islamic traditional peacemaking culture for help, rather than to Islam. They did not jettison Islam, but they discerned in their traditional pre-Islamic systems of restorative justice resources that they hoped would be especially helpful.

Somalis often say that both religion and culture are powerful, but the most powerful is culture. Leaders came to recognize that the pre-Islamic tradition of restorative justice, or *xeer*, had much to offer in the peacemaking process. It was to that traditional foundation that I turned as I reentered Somalia with a specific mandate to work at peacemaking. As a Christian committed to restorative justice, I found some common ground and significant similarities between pre-Islamic Somali approaches to peacemaking and the Old Testament and New Testament visions of shalom.

In my role as a consultant I knew that I would need to build upon these pre-Islamic peacemaking themes within my society as we worked at inter-clan peace within the Somali conflict. *Nabad*—or peace—is the traditional Somali greeting. Yet peace must be centered in justice, and justice proceeds from God. The traditional name for God is Waaq. When the rains are ample, the grazing abundant, and there is peace, this is referred to as *Barwaaqo*, meaning the place of God (*Bar*—place; *Waaq*—God). Wherever God is present there is nabad. This is why nabad is the everyday Somali greeting reflecting both personal and community well-being. It has similarities to the Old Testament concept of shalom.

In traditional culture, when there is an injustice and the wise elders have gathered to determine justice, they will advise the offenders and victims, *"Gar Waaq."* *Gar* means chin. It is by the chin that the herdsman guides his camel. So the protagonists are advised to accept the judge leading them by the chin to the justice of God. That is, the responsibility of the elders is to lead the protagonists to justice. They may also say *"Gar Waaq so"* or "Take God's justice, not mine or ours." In fact, the judge is called *gar sore*, meaning the one who serves justice. So the judge is the one who serves or leads, not the one who judges. Ultimately, God is the judge, and the function of the human judge is only to lead the assembled elders to discernment in regard to the justice of God. Although the elders have counseled, justice is from God, so they commend those who have come to the court to submit to the justice of God.

Both the aggrieved party and the offender meet before the judge whose responsibility it is to lead the two to accept the justice of God. This includes decisions about appropriate payments for the restoration of justice. The offender will offer the number of animals that have been determined as just payment for the offense. If it is not a mortal offense, in magnanimity the victim will redistribute the livestock he has received. He redistributes in equal portions to the offender and his clan leaders as well as to himself and his or her own clan leaders. Then both parties will slay a portion of the redistributed livestock and have a feast together. This is xeer! This is a covenant of restorative justice.

In my clan, when a person is accused of an injustice and comes before the gathering for judgment, he will say that he is "giving his head." After the matter has been decided, the one accused presents his substitutionary sacrifice, usually a lamb. Then the head of the person charged with wrong doing is restored through the substitutionary offering. When the lamb is sacrificed for peacemaking, it is referred to as *Waaq dhacan*—literally, God dies or God has fallen. Likewise when the lamb is hung up it is referred to as hanging up God. By eating the lamb together, both the victim and offender seal the covenant of peace that is possible after the aggrieved are satisfied that justice has been done. This covenant for forgiveness is also an expression of xeer.

Christ in lively engagement with traditional peacemaking

A French anthropologist, René Girard, observes that within all traditional religions animal or human sacrifice is always offered when there is a commitment to reconciliation and restoration. The sacrificial animal must be perfect and innocent of the causes of the conflict. In slaying the sacrificial animal, the protagonists are hurling their hostility against the innocent victim who absorbs the hostility without taking revenge. Both the aggrieved victim and the perpetrator of the grievance project their grievance and hostility upon the innocent victim. The sacrifice is often perceived as the embodiment of divinity. God or the gods is identified with the sacrifice. By absorbing the violence, the victim thereby breaks the cycles of violence and retribution. In this way the innocent victim brings a restoration of peace. The peace is effectuated through a covenant wherein the protagonists join together in eating the flesh of the sacrificial victim.

Girard believes that these sacrifices for restoration of peace are a prototype that is fulfilled in Christ, the Lamb of God. He is the best that heaven or humanity can offer. He is innocent of the violence hurled upon him on the cross. He is the divine sacrifice who absorbs the hostility and forgives, thereby bringing reconciliation. At the communion table the reconciled community partakes of bread and wine, symbols of the body and blood of Christ. The communion table with the bread and wine are signs of the cross and resurrection of Christ confirming the believer's participation in the covenant of reconciliation with God and others.[1]

I agree with Girard's insightful observation on the role of sacrifice in effectuating reconciliation. Among my people in the sacrifice of the animal, God himself is identifying with that sacrifice. Justice, forgiveness, and restoration are indeed costly! I see all these themes, within the traditional approaches to justice and restoration, as signs that are fulfilled in Jesus the Lamb of God and his sacrificial death on the cross for our sin. I believe that the covenant of peace that is sealed in eating the sacrificial lamb together is a sign that is fulfilled in the covenant signified by the communion table of the Lord.

In my peacemaking efforts within the Somali context, I make linkages between the cross of Christ and the traditional themes. I believe that the sacrifice of animals is a sign of restoration of peace, but in itself is incapable of authentically transforming the inner wellsprings of hostility and hatred within the person. The real restoration that goes to the root causes of strife within the human heart is centered in the cross and resurrection of Christ and the healing work of the Holy Spirit.

Networking for peacemaking

My commitment to peacemaking, therefore, is Christ-centered, and I vigorously commend the non-violent way of Christ. However, most of those I work with have not embraced a Christ-centered approach to peacemaking; in fact, they believe that Jesus was astonishingly impractical. They draw from values and insights from Islam or pre-Islamic beliefs. I do not disparage values from other streams of spirituality or wisdom from the ancient sages. Neither do I impose my Christ-centered peacemaking commitments on those who are not committed to the way of the cross that is so central to the peace of Christ.

Still, I vigorously network with all who are devoted to seeking conflict transformation among the Somali people. It is for this reason that for those three months I focused on networking with clan leaders who were committed to finding a way to end the violent hostilities. A variety of agencies, such as MCC and Ergo, stood with me as we sought to develop and maintain communication bridges between those involved in the conflict. Sometimes I well nigh despaired; yet in hope I pressed onward.

Called as a peace ambassador to Somalia

I returned to the United States in June 1991 for a time of reprieve and to reconnect with my family. A month later we welcomed the birth of our daughter, Sofia. We were indeed a blessed family! We also knew that God's calling for ongoing engagement with Somalia was compelling. So I occupied myself with a variety of employments awaiting God's timing for our return to Somalia.

In September, World Concern, a humanitarian nongovernmental organization, contacted us about a possible assignment working with Somalis in East Africa. We pursued that option with some seriousness. We hoped that World Concern might provide a niche for us and provide a forum for me to work at my peacemaking commitments. I did not imagine that these preliminary contacts with World Concern would be crucial in saving my life four months later.

Only a month later I received another urgent invitation from the clan elders for me to return to Somalia. We knew that the answer had to be "Yes!" Within days of the invitation, I was on my way back to Somalia.

I left on October 20, 1991, and returned to the United States on January 26, 1992. We originally thought I would be gone for two weeks! Alas, I was gone for another three months. For the first month Martha and I had occasional phone contact. Then communication came to a halt as the forces of disintegration took hold. It helped immensely that Martha had lived and worked in Somalia before. Still, it was a distressing time for her. When Thanksgiving came I was not there. Christmas, and still no word. She contacted the American State Department, but since I carried a Somali passport they could do nothing. Martha was exceedingly concerned.

I knew what I was doing, but Martha knew nothing. She only knew that I was engaged in a dangerous mission. Not only had communication between Somalia and the outside world been severed; the warlord Mohamed Farrah Aidid had also closed the airport. Relief and development agencies had migrated to Nairobi.

In December 1992—just a year after I had returned to Mogadishu—an American and United Nations military intervention was to begin. Even that massive military intervention would not control the strife. Ten months later, in October 1993, a catastrophic crash of U.S. Black Hawk helicopters would leave Somalia horrifically emblazoned in the memories of Americans.

But at the end of 1991, I was engaged in a very different intervention. I, along with others, was unobtrusively shuttling between warlords. In my previous visit, fellow peacemakers and I had met one of the most powerful militia commanders, Mohamed Farrah Aidid. We had met in May in the town of Jilib. He used the occasion to give a rambling lecture on international agencies and democracy. That encounter convinced me that attempts to influence or coerce warlords such as Aidid were futile. I had a sense of the minefields within the political terrain. I feared that international intervention would be like pouring oil on fire.

This time, when I had first arrived in Mogadishu, the interim government had invited me to be assistant minister for foreign affairs. One of my clan elders said that they were engaged in a soccer game and my sub-clan wanted me at the center of the game. Of course that was a metaphor of their political maneuvering. I declined. I felt that I would have greater maneuverability in peacemaking working unobtrusively outside the political system.

My plan was that each clan faction would have representatives within a representative council—the kind of network we had been developing in my previous three months in Mogadishu. So now I worked with a team of elders who were following up contacts. An inter-clan council was developing some momentum. We were also forming an advisory council of peacemakers who were consultants rather than political power brokers. We saw some glimmers of hope. Aidid, however, was not impressed.

A rocket attack

On January 12, Mohamed Farah Aidid's militia shot a rocket-propelled grenade over the wall into the courtyard where a number of us peacemakers were holding discussions. I was the target. I did not see the grenade coming. It missed my upper body, but exploded as it crashed into my leg, just below the knee. Those around me took a knife and severed my leg. There was no anesthesia. As I lost consciousness, I saw my body below me. I was experiencing an out-of-body phenomenon. Death was beckoning.

My friends moved me to a house in the "Bermuda Triangle" section of Mogadishu by wheelbarrow. The Bermuda Triangle got its notorious name from an earlier military excursion launched by Aidid when his troops and military equipment were "swallowed." Thereafter this region of the city was considered to be the vortex of death. I lay there from Sunday to Friday. Then they moved me by Land Rover to a house in another section of the city known as Karaan. Those around me assumed I was awaiting death.

There was no medical care. The pain was horrific. A bloody rag covered my wounded stump providing some protection from the flies. I hovered between consciousness and unconsciousness. Then I remembered my leg.

"Go find my leg!" I commanded my colleagues.

"Your leg is buried!" they told me.

"I must have my leg. Get it now!"

My nephew followed my instructions and brought the severed leg.

I urged him, "Look in the sock that is still on the foot."

Sure enough, it was still there. My money, three hundred and fifteen dollars! I had placed the money in my sock for safekeeping. I would need that money to leave the country, if the opportunity ever came. Fortunately, I had also kept my documents with me, in my clothing.

My brother in Christ, Mohammed Sheikh Don, lived in another area of the city. His clan was in violent conflict with my clan. Yet, the moment the rocket exploded, several colleagues became emissaries and ran across the city to report to Sheikh Don, "Your friend has been wounded."

Immediately he set out across that treacherous city to find me. Alas, when he got to the battle lines, the fighters would not let him cross to see me. They said, "We know your brother is wounded, but you cannot go to see him."

Although Mohammed could not meet me, by sundown that day the whole city knew that he had tried to cross the battle lines to meet me, his brother in the faith. His quest to meet me at great risk to his life was a banner of witness in that wounded city: believers in Christ are bonded in a brotherly love that transcends clan identities.

The days crept by tediously. A week passed with no help on the horizon. I knew that without a dramatic intervention I would die. My trip to Somalia had been at the request of the Somali people; no agency had sponsored this trip. Ergo had endorsed the trip, but they had no organization or personnel in the region. So no one knew who to contact. The days were long and the nights difficult. "How long, oh Lord?" I prayed.

Rescued by an ambulance plane

Some days into my plight I had revived sufficiently to think about who might be in a position to help. It had occurred to me that World Concern, which had been negotiating with us for a possible East Africa assignment, might consider extending a helping hand. So I took a taxi across town to the Red Cross headquarters. I urged the Red Cross to get word to World Concern in Nairobi that I had been wounded. When the news of my plight finally got to World Concern, they immediately arranged for an African Medical and Research Foundation (AMREF) plane to retrieve me from Mogadishu.

In the meantime a Somali called Martha from Mogadishu. She was on her way to church on Sunday morning when the call came. When she heard that I was alive although wounded, she

wept. The caller rebuked her, "Thousands are dying in Mogadishu. Your husband is still alive. So why do you cry?"

This abrupt statement by the unknown caller really shook
Martha and caused her to view the situation from a perspective
of gratitude to God for sparing my life, while still lamenting my
injury. She received the news that I was still alive as a special gift
from God; it came just before her birthday celebration.

Eleven days after my leg had been severed I was hoisted into
the AMREF ambulance plane for the two-hour flight to Nairobi. I arrived in Nairobi Thursday afternoon, January 23. World
Concern leaders, Michael Madney and Craig Anderson, met me
at the airport. Then, for the first time in eleven days I received
professional medical care. The next morning Harold Miller and
others from the Mennonite team who were serving with MCC
and EMM in Nairobi came to the hospital. These colleagues
donated the blood that I desperately needed. I was hospitalized
another night and then placed on a stretcher for the flight to
Amsterdam and then Chicago. A World Concern nurse accompanied me all the way.

The medical prognosis: you will die

I arrived in Chicago on January 26, 1992. Ed Wenzler from
Eastbrook Church was there with his van, along with Pastor
Marc Erickson. But most importantly, Martha and the children,
Afrah and Sofia, were there, along with Martha's sister. We all
wept in thanksgiving. The van drove straight to one of the lead-
ing hospitals in Milwaukee where I was admitted immediately.

A top medical team explored the wounded leg and performed
various tests. Several days later the lab results showed that a
pernicious infection had penetrated my leg stump. It was known
as necrotizing fasciitis. The doctors cut one portion after another off my stump to try to get ahead of the infection, but they
could not stop it. Five times they sawed off segments of the leg.

Then they put me in a sealed decompression chamber for
hyperbaric treatment. The air in the chamber is highly oxyge-
nized with high pressure akin to some sixty feet under water.
This is to kill the bacteria because the bacteria cannot tolerate

oxygen. It becomes exceedingly cold. It was terrible. I begged the doctors to stop!

As far as the doctors could discern, the treatment did not seem to have worked. There was nothing more they could do; all three doctors told me that unless God intervened miraculously, I would die. I needed to put my house in order and bid my family and friends farewell. I was prepared to die. However, hundreds joined in intercessory prayer beseeching the Great Physician to intervene. The nurses thought I must be a VIP because I was getting so many cards from all over the world.

"Who are you?" they asked in bewilderment.

Divine intervention

Then the Lord spoke through my friend Philip Accad, who was from Lebanon but living in Milwaukee. The day after my treatment, Philip came to my hospital bedside with his young son and Marc Erickson. Philip said, "When I was in prayer for you, the Lord spoke saying, 'Ahmed will not die. I will raise Ahmed up and restore his health for I still have ministry for him to do in Africa.'"

We bowed in prayers of thanksgiving. What more could I say, except to thank the Lord for his promise that I would live? That was on Saturday morning. That same morning when the doctors inspected the wound, they found no infection! All lab tests came back negative. The doctors were astonished.

The doctors told me, "We have found only healthy tissue. The deadly process is completely gone. You will live!" My doctors observed that this was certainly a miracle and that they could not take credit for my healing.

I was released from the hospital a month later, on February 28, 1992.

On my first excursion outside the hospital, Martha asked me, "What do you want to eat?"

I said, "Ice cream!—and chicken."

CHAPTER 8

Foundation
for Peacemaking
Expanding Horizons
(1992–94)

Your attitude should be the same, as that of Christ Jesus.
—Apostle Paul

THE next months were filled with giving presentations related to Christian engagement with Islam in peacemaking. In May a large meeting convened in Toronto, organized by Ergo, the group that had been so encouraging of my trips to Somalia. We Somalis are a noisy crowd, so there was a lot of shouting at that meeting. Some non-Somali participants were perplexed by the boisterous and apparently angry shouting. But that is the way we Somalis vent our frustrations; we shout at each other. So it was a good meeting!

We realized that we could not be helpful in peacemaking in Somalia if we were not working together. Most of the key leaders in the Ergo movement had been influenced by the Mennonite presence and schools in Somalia. Sometimes they were nicknamed the Muslim Mennonites. They contributed to the discussions with a conciliatory spirit.

One of the serendipitous outcomes of Ergo has been Mennonite Central Committee (MCC) and Eastern Mennonite Missions (EMM) support for elders peacemaking councils in Somalia. This is exactly what I had worked so hard to see develop in Mogadishu. The councils of elders as they emerged have been more effective in regions some distance from the political tensions in Mogadishu. These councils have contributed in helpful ways to some of the peacemaking developments in a variety of regions of Somalia, and especially in the north.

Encounter with Somalis in Sweden

While I was in the hospital I had received an invitation from the Lutheran Evangelical Fellowship of Sweden (EFS) to attend a series of consultations related to the growing Somali community in Sweden. I said I would come only if Martha, Afrah, and Sofia could accompany me. They agreed. So in June, right after the Ergo gathering in Toronto, we boarded a plane for Stockholm where we attended a large gathering of the EFS. Then we went on to Uppsala for a general assembly of the Swedish Lutheran Church. This was a large gathering in a cathedral with a lot of pomp; this was rather strange for us who were used to more casual gatherings of church leaders. After this we met with some Somali leaders.

That October I returned to Sweden with three colleagues from Ergo to the southern city of Lune for meetings with the Somalis there. Since the conflict in Somalia had extended into relationships among Somalis in Sweden, the gatherings were tendentious and tumultuous. Feelings ran very deep and anger exploded! I asked them why they were fighting with each other. They explained that it was because they were supporting different clan leaders in Somalia, each represented among the Somali diaspora in Sweden. Then I told them that there were no authentic leaders in Somalia, for all the so-called leaders were fighting with each other. This quieted them down. I also challenged them to see their role as Somalis in the diaspora as one of making peace, not fanning the flames of hostility. In response a person in the audience gave me a riddle to solve: "If, among you four Ergo representatives, there were only three plates of food, how would you divide the food?"

This was my resolution of the riddle: "One plate would go to my colleague, Ali, who is from one clan. The second plate would go to my colleague, Osman, from another clan. The third plate I would divide with Sofia who is of my clan. We can do it that way, or we can fight so that in the end all the food is spoiled and wasted."

They laughed and got the point. That helped to break the hostility. Then they were open to our suggestions on how they might transform the hostility between their clans and work for peacemaking.

A whirlwind of speaking engagements

Toronto and Uppsala were just the beginning of many engagements and presentations on peace. In July 1992 I spoke at a gathering of Franciscans in Burlington, Wisconsin. In October I went to Winnipeg, Manitoba, to speak at a Mennonite colleges' peace consortium. Then in Kidron, Ohio, I addressed the MCC Great Lakes annual meeting. In November we were invited to speak at Charlotte Street (now called James Street) Mennonite Church in Lancaster, Pennsylvania. That turned out to be an important connection, for there were a number of people in that congregation who had served in Somalia, and they were eager to encourage networking with us in our ministry.

Also in November I, along with others, formed the Somali Conservation Corps, a group interested in conserving the Somali natural environment through peacemaking. Desertification makes human life unsustainable and is the fuel of conflict. This tragedy is caused by overgrazing and cutting trees for charcoal manufacturing. Our vision was to work with youth interested in peacemaking by demobilizing the militia active in clan warfare, while at the same time challenging and mobilizing these youth to put their energies into conservation of arable land.

For about a year I had worked on developing this vision with Marc Erickson's encouragement. The idea had come to us from Doug Coe who was leader of the Fellowship in Washington, D.C., which sponsors the annual Presidential Prayer Breakfast. Doug was keen about the proposal that I had developed. Marc Erickson accompanied me as did colleagues from the Fellowship: Cortez Ragland and Jim Kielsmeirer.

The plan would initially be centered in the Bulo Burte district.

A UNO plane took us from Nairobi to the Karaan section of Mogadishu where we met with Somali leaders to plan for ways to implement the plan. (Two years later, in 1994, I was involved in a follow-up trip. We had acquired a $300,000 grant from CARE. This time the UNO plane took us to Bulo Burte, and the proposal was well received. However, just as we were developing connections and testing the vision, another of Somalia's inter-clan conflicts exploded, and we had to send an SOS to the UNO to send a plane and get us safely back to Nairobi.)

In February and March, 1993, I traveled on another mission into the Horn of Africa—this time to participate in the Addis Peace Forum in Addis Ababa, Ethiopia, which was jointly sponsored by the Life and Peace Institute in Sweden and UNOSAM, a UNO effort at peacemaking in Somalia. This was a substantial effort to bring Somali elders and decision-makers together to explore peacemaking in Somalia.

Preparing to return to Somalia

Amidst all of this, Martha had completed her degree at AMBS with an MA in theology. Then we moved to Terre Haute, Indiana, where Martha could continue graduate studies in church history at Indiana State University. Professor Robert Clouse was a key resource, for he had written extensively on Christian views of war.[1] That was important for Martha because her church tradition had not exposed her to peace theology. She reveled in her studies in church history and especially sixteenth and seventeenth century developments in the Christian movement. Over the years, we had used every opportunity to strengthen our academic credentials. We both had studied at Indiana State University as well as AMBS. Our combined areas of study were richly pertinent to our commitment to the Somali people: peacemaking, political science, church history, and theology.

The years 1992 and 1993 were also a special time of developing a network of churches and individuals who would stand with us in prayer, encouragement, and financial support whenever the door would open for our return to East Africa. We had not squandered the six years invested in the United States after our 1988 departure from Somalia. These years provided strategic opportunities to bear witness to the gospel within the North American context. We also knew that whenever the door would open to return to ministry among the Somali people, we were determined to go as faithful ambassadors of Jesus the Messiah who is the Prince of Peace. How would we bear witness to that message as we ventured back into East African and Somali societies?

What is the message of peace?

There are many ideologies and theologies of peacemaking. Even Marxism proclaims an ideology of peacemaking. As disciples of Jesus Christ, we are committed to Christ-centered peacemaking. The peace of Christ is different than the peace of Islam or the traditional Somali Nabad. In fact, the peace of Christ is not the same as any of the alternative varieties of peace throughout the world.

I believe the gospel of Jesus Christ provides a unique and revolutionary gift within the realms of peacemaking. To say this is not to deny the value of studying the techniques for peacemaking and conflict transformation, drawn from the disciplines of sociology and psychology. Many of my courses at AMBS focused in those directions. As I showed in the previous chapter, there is also value in exploring peacemaking themes within Islam or traditional religions. Those themes can be helpful but also have their inadequacies, as is true of all peacemaking techniques.

However, Jesus Christ invites us to move far beyond techniques of conflict transformation and to meet Jesus crucified and risen. The cross is distinct and revolutionary. In Christ crucified, the God of the universe suffers and dies for us and forgives. In his crucifixion and resurrection, Jesus decisively breaks the cycles of retributive justice. He invites us into the forgiving and reconciling embrace of God. No philosophy or religion has ever imagined that God could love that much. The call of God upon my life is to be a faithful ambassador of Jesus Christ and the truly healing peace he offers.

Islam denies the cross, for Islam does not fathom that God could love that much. My many Muslim friends believe that the cross is a betrayal of the power and sovereignty of God. Indeed, in Islam Jesus the Messiah is rescued from the cross and taken to heaven without dying. But it is not just Islam that finds the cross unfathomable. Even in my presentations to North American Christian audiences (such as those described earlier) I sometimes meet people who are astonished that God really does love that much.

In chapter three I described the life-giving transformation I experienced at the Word of Life Camp outside Nairobi just after leaving Mogadishu in 1973. As I mentioned, my change in worldview was grounded in a Bible study based on Philippians 2:1-11. In that passage, Paul writes,

> Your attitude should be the same as that of Christ Jesus: Who, being in very nature God, did not consider equality with God something to be grasped, but made himself nothing, taking the very nature of a servant, being made in human likeness. And being found in appearance as a man, he humbled himself and became obedient to death— even death on a cross! Therefore God has highly exalted him to the highest place and gave him a name that is above every name, that at the name of Jesus every knee should bow, in heaven and on earth and under the earth, and every tongue confess that Jesus Christ is Lord, to the glory of God the Father. (Philippians 2:5-11)

At the Word of Life Camp, the Holy Spirit revealed that the cross is not weakness but rather the transforming power of the love of God. We discover that when all else fails there is the cross. Only the cross goes to the heart of the matter, namely our alienation from God and one another. When we bear witness to that reality, our presence and witness becomes a healing presence among the nations, including the Somali people and global Islam. This is true even though the community of those who believe in Jesus as Savior and Lord might be a very small community. Jesus said where two or three meet in his name, he is present (Matthew 18:20).

That takes us to the church. The gospel is not just revolutionary theology—although it most certainly is that—it is much more. Jesus Christ was committed to forming a reconciled people. After his death and resurrection, a new people was formed through the empowerment of the Holy Spirit. The Scriptures as penned by Paul describe this people as a community of reconciliation:

> For he himself is our peace, who has made the two one and has destroyed the barrier, the dividing wall of hostility,...and in this one body to reconcile both of them to God through the cross, by which he put to death their hostility. (Ephesians 2:14-16)

The Somali nation is one of only a tiny handful of states in Africa who comprise one people and one language. With rare exceptions, all Somalis are Sunni Muslim. Yet this common ethnic, linguistic, and religious glue has not been sufficient to mitigate the countervailing forces of clan identity. This is why I refuse to even name my clan in these memoirs. We must find an identity that can transcend clan loyalties. For me that identity is the church. The faithful church in its very essence is a community of reconciliation.

In the passage just cited, Paul recognizes that the Ephesian church was born within a context of destructive inter-ethnic and inter-religious hostility between Jews and Gentiles. The hostility was so deep that the two groups would not even eat together. However, for those who had received the gift of reconciliation offered in Jesus the Messiah, crucified and risen, God was creating a new and reconciled humanity. This reconciled humanity was a miracle. That is why I stand within the church in all my efforts in peacemaking. As Paul writes,

> All of this is from God, who reconciled us to himself through Christ and gave us the ministry of reconciliation: that God was reconciling the world to himself in Christ, not counting men's sins against them. And he has committed to us the message of reconciliation. We are therefore Christ's ambassadors, as though God were making his appeal through us. We implore you on Christ's behalf: Be reconciled to God. (2 Corinthians 5:18-21)

I consider it an honor of the highest order to be called of God to be an ambassador of the gospel of reconciliation. I identify with Paul who exclaimed in amazement that God had called him! He writes, "But by the grace of God I am what I am, and his grace to me was not without effect. No, I worked harder than all of them—yet not I, but the grace of God that was with me" (1 Corinthians 15:9-10). The ambassador of a nation seeks to represent his country with excellence. By God's grace I have yearned to be an excellent ambassador for Jesus Christ and his kingdom, to be a true and faithful emissary of the gospel of peace.

Through the empowerment of the Holy Spirit, the gospel of reconciliation brings about a new reconciled creation. That new creation is characterized by ethical commitments that are centered in the way of the cross. My ambassadorial ethical commitments were proclaimed by Jesus in what is known as the Sermon on the Mount (Matthew 5–7). Here are several especially pertinent excerpts:

> Blessed are the peacemakers, for they will be called the sons of God. (Matthew 5:9)

> You have heard that it was said, "Eye for eye, and tooth for tooth." But I tell you, Do not resist an evil person. If someone strikes you on the right cheek, turn to him the other also. And if someone wants to sue you and take your tunic, let him have your cloak as well. If someone forces you to go one mile, go with him two miles. Give to the one who asks you, and do not turn away from the one who wants to borrow from you. (Matthew 5:38-42)

> You have heard that it was said, "Love your neighbor, and hate your enemy." But I tell you: Love your enemies and pray for those who persecute you, that you may be sons of your Father in heaven. (Matthew 5:43-44)

As we read the epistles, which are letters of counsel and instruction to the newly forming churches, we gain insights on the practical outworking of what it means for the church to be a community of reconciliation. Romans 12 has been very important in shaping me; it has been as an ethical manifesto for our family:

Bless those who persecute you; bless and do not curse. Rejoice with those who rejoice; mourn with those who mourn. Live in harmony with one another. Do not be proud, but be willing to associate with people of low position. Do not be conceited.

Do not repay anyone evil for evil. Be careful to do what is right in the eyes of everybody. If it is possible, as far as it depends on you, live in peace with everyone. Do not take revenge, my friends, but leave room for God's wrath, for it is written: "It is mine to avenge; I will repay," says the Lord. On the contrary: "If your enemy is hungry, feed him; if he is thirsty, give him something to drink. In doing this, you will heap burning coals on his head." Do not be overcome by evil, but overcome evil with good. (Romans 12:14-21)

Only those among whom we have lived can assess the extent to which we have really lived this way—but this has been our goal. Within all our imperfections and stumbles, we are grateful that Christ has called us to be ambassadors of the gospel of reconciliation! The essence of that calling has become increasingly clear to me. As Paul puts it, my yearning is to bear witness to Christ crucified and risen, who is the power of God (1 Corinthians 2:2). I believe that Jesus is, to use a phrase from Henri Nouwen's book by the same name, the Wounded Healer.

Invited to East Africa

As 1993 came to a close, we were blessed with a third child, Gedi. Martha's last examination at Indiana State University was December 17. Two days later on December 19 Gedi was born. This Christmastime baby filled our home with joy. Afrah (five years) and Sofia (two years) loved their baby brother.

As an added blessing, within months of Gedi's birth an invitation to return to East Africa finally came our way. We would be jointly appointed by Eastern Mennonite Missions and Mennonite Central Committee and live in Nairobi. Martha and I would teach at Daystar University. I was told I could be assigned to teach courses on Islam as well, although the Muslim community in Kenya was quite skittish about a former Muslim doing that. I knew that part of such an assignment would have to be building trust with the Muslim community.

We had a strong network of support. Eastbrook Church in Milwaukee, ever faithful, committed substantial funds as did Charlotte Street (now James Street) Mennonite Church in Lancaster and Assembly Mennonite Church in Goshen. Both MCC and EMM partnered in program oversight as well as program funding. These churches and agencies were also committed to prayer, not just financial support. Then there were also the many individual friends who contributed and prayed for us. They were committed to our family and to our calling to be ambassadors of the gospel of peace.

With high expectations, we left for Nairobi on July 18, 1994. We had not imagined the challenges that were before us as we returned to East Africa. Within weeks we would be embroiled in conflict.

CHAPTER 9

Hope Within Conflict
Somali Church and Daystar University
(1994–2009)

Seek peace and pursue it.
—Apostle Peter

Upon our arrival in Nairobi, our primary assignment was Daystar University, which was a rapidly developing pan-Africa Christian university. The student enrollment then was close to seven hundred students; today it is about three thousand. Completely separate from our university commitments was our yearning to be involved with the emerging fellowship of Somali believers in Christ. So when the administration of the university invited us to join the faculty, I made it clear that a priority for us would also be to build and encourage the Somali church. The administration of the university fully supported that commitment.

At that time there was a Somali congregation of about twenty or thirty participants. Furthermore, missionaries had developed a dynamic residential discipleship training program with about a dozen Somali young men participating. The anticipation of teaching within this discipleship training center delighted me. I had never engaged in this kind of ministry.

Conflict in the church

One reason for my enthusiasm for this discipleship training center was my memory of the decisive way that the Word of Life

Camp had formed me as a twenty-year-old Somali refugee. Now, twenty years later, young refugee Somali men were experiencing spiritual transformation in the training program. While still in the United States, I envisaged the joy of investing in the lives of these young men. After my arrival the two missionary leaders of the center invited me to teach leadership. I was exhilarated and I prepared well for this class.

Alas, as I began teaching, a terrible conflict exploded right within the class. We Somalis can be quite volatile; two of the participants came to blows. The class was in uproar. I did my best to dampen the flames. So this was our discipleship training school! I was dismayed. Since the participants in the school were also in the church, the tensions spread into the church. Consequently the two expatriate leaders decided to close both the school and the church.

I was deeply angered. As far as I know, the Somalis in the church had not been consulted. The missionaries were not the Somali church; the church is the church. It is called to be a community of reconciliation. Therefore, my deep conviction is that when strife occurs, the way forward cannot be to close the church. Instead, the way of Jesus is to address the roots of the strife, repent, forgive, be reconciled, receive the transforming gift of the Holy Spirit, and move forward. The conflict in the church was tragic and wrong. Yet the strife presented a profoundly teachable moment to learn together what it means to be a community of forgiveness and reconciliation. That could never happen if the church was closed and ceased to meet. How could the church be a beacon for reconciliation and peace when there was no peace in the church?

My counsel could not be heard. Some missionaries advised that my assignment in Nairobi was as a professor at Daystar, not involvement in the church. I should leave the Somali church matters to missionaries appointed to work with the church, it seemed, and not meddle in their affairs. I should worship elsewhere and not with the Somali church. This suggestion astonished me. Years before, I had struggled with Muslim leaders of Mogadishu for inclusion within the Muslim community. Now I was struggling for inclusion within the Somali church!

I confronted the missionaries. "I am a Somali and I cannot go back into my mother's womb and be born someone else!" I told them, kindly but firmly. "I am a member of the church. In all my years in Somalia I have been actively committed to the Somali church. When I moved to Nairobi from Somalia twenty years ago, I was committed to the church, including the Somali expression of the church. I will not accept that you have the authority to exclude me from the Somali church. The church belongs to Christ, not to you missionaries. You do not have the authority to exclude me."

As I mentioned, we Somalis can be divisive in our relations with one another. Some of the Somalis sided with the missionaries and urged me to desist from worshipping with Somali believers. I grieved that Somali factionalism and volatile individualism contributed to the scattering and disintegration of the Somali Believers Fellowship in Nairobi.

The vision for the church

Sometime after the conflict a Swiss brother, Siegfried, and I began to meet for prayer every Wednesday morning at 6:00 a.m. In time others joined us. Week by week we prayed for the Somali church. Within a year believers began to gather again. Some who had scattered when the church was closed never came back, but others did return, and some brought new believers with them. With joy and expectation, we witnessed the Holy Spirit bringing about the renewal of the church.

The development of a church composed of believers of Somali Muslim background was in harmony with the vision we had in Eastleigh twenty years earlier. Now, two decades later, there was a growing Somali church in Nairobi. This was a fulfillment of that early vision. Martha and I would not be detracted from commitment to the Somali fellowship of believers.

The Somali Believers Fellowship began to convene again, this time at a location closer to our home. However, in recognition of the diversities of the mission agencies working with the church, we often changed locations, meeting sometimes on the premises of one agency and then another. Sometimes the fellowship met in our home. It was a joy to see children come to the gathering; they sang with all their might, often clapping or drumming on tables and dancing as they rejoiced in the gift of salvation in Jesus.

Islamist opposition

Commitment to the Somali church involved risks. I was well known among Islamists, and some threatened to hurt me. Twenty years earlier I had lived in Eastleigh, the predominantly Somali-Muslim area of the city. We had lived across the street from the Sufi mosque on Eighth Street and occasionally had meals together with the Muslim leadership. Those days were now a nostalgic memory. With the turmoil in Somalia and the absence of political authority, jihadist Islam was taking root in Somalia and the influence of militant Islam was penetrating Eastleigh.

My friends told me that occasionally sermons in mosques explicitly accused me of inciting Muslims to become Christians. There were threats against my life, even in broadcasts from Radio Mogadishu. So I rarely ventured into Eastleigh. Although most of the members of the growing Somali fellowship came from Eastleigh, we always met in other areas of the city.

However, I did go to Eastleigh when I felt that my presence would contribute to peacemaking. Such engagements were important in my commitment to building bridges instead of walls. I determined never to let fear determine my commitments. I knew that the Lord had raised me from near death at least twice—from the cerebral malaria in Bulo Burte and the necrotizing fasciitis in Milwaukee. My life belonged to Christ. Nothing could assail me that was outside his shepherding care.

If my calling to be an ambassador of the gospel of reconciliation resulted in death, I was quite ready to accept that calling for the sake of Christ. I would never kill, for I was captivated by the redemptive suffering love revealed in his crucifixion. The Somali jihadists would wear a white burial cloth around their heads as a sign of their readiness to die for their cause. For me, the white cloth symbolizes my death in Christ. My burial cloth is the cross of Christ. I was ready to die for Jesus, for I knew that in my identification with him, I would arise from the dead as he did, and serve him forever in his kingdom. So death carried no fear for me. I was careful and aware of my surroundings, but not controlled by fear because of threats coming from Eastleigh or Mogadishu.

The consequences of all the criticism against me and against the ministries I was engaged in were not all negative. On one occasion Radio Mogadishu invested a couple of hours just on me. This led people to believe I was a very important person indeed. Furthermore, the radio hosts described in some detail the ministries I was engaged in, such as teaching peace studies at a very important university in Nairobi. And they told about our involvement in the church and how Somalis were becoming believers. Somalis were surprised that such an important person from a prominent family in Somalia would be investing himself so energetically in the church. Ironically, therefore, the broadcasts fed a growing interest in the gospel and the church.

Challenges to the unity of church

We Somalis are individualists. That independent spirit always affected the church in Nairobi. Sometimes there would be one large fellowship; at other times we would fracture into several smaller fellowships. Sometimes I was affirmed as a leader, and at other times I was not. We experienced many challenges to our ongoing unity in Christ.

However, a wonderful highlight of our church life was our semi-annual retreats, when believers would come together for fellowship and study. The retreats were held on the outskirts of Nairobi. The group consisted mostly of Somalis, Somali-Kenyans, and Somali refugees. The refugees were always very concerned about police raids, harassments, jailings, and deportations. The retreats provided four days of reprieve through fellowship, teaching, worship, and fun. The Bible studies and other teaching provided spiritual nourishment. Our memories of those retreats continue to encourage and challenge us.

The struggle with some agencies

The tensions in the discipleship program and the church, alluded to earlier in the chapter, were not only related to our Somali inclination toward unstable group relations; they were also influenced by the missionaries related to the various agencies working among Somalis in Kenya. Reaching back into Somalia itself, in the 1950s and '60s, there were both the Somalia Mennonite Mission and the Sudan Interior Mission. These missions maintained cordial relations, yet it was unavoidable that there emerged two different groups of Somali believers, with respective loyalties to the two missions. In Nairobi these different missions continued relating to the Somali believers. They encouraged unity, yet unity was not always experienced. Some of the appointees of these missions were especially committed to peace and justice concerns, and others emphasized evangelism. I believe that these commitments were complementary, and in fact the Somali church believed in the integration of peacemaking and evangelism.

However, in Kenya inter-agency dynamics could become quite complex. Agencies and churches became involved that had no historic memory of SIM and SMM or of MCC and EMM. Several church groups seemed to have independent sectarian inclinations. Some had just recently arrived in Kenya and viewed the Somali church as the community meriting their special focus. We wept sometimes at the ways some agencies and sects pulled the believers in different directions. A couple of groups approached us offering their help. We welcomed all the help we could get. The next thing we knew, however, some were attempting to sabotage our authority.

For example, the Somali leadership, along with the missionary partners whom they trusted, worked slowly at baptism. In contrast, one especially grievous development was the decision of one of these newly arrived groups to baptize all the believers. They were in a hurry. With no consultation and never informing us, they secretly baptized the believers. We were not invited and knew nothing about their plans. All the baptismal candidates, who were mostly women, were asked to dress in light-weight, white baptismal gowns. When they entered the water, the gowns clung to their bodies. An event that should have been one of great joy turned into shame. The women later said that they were so humiliated that they urinated in the water in which they were baptized. Back in Eastleigh the word about the shameful ritual spread among their Muslim neighbors.

While we were concerned about Islamic militancy during our years in Nairobi, one of our greatest challenges was coping with some of these Christian groups who came to Kenya to "help" us.

Encouraging the church

I want to stress here that a number of the individuals and agencies did function with noteworthy sensitivity. They were genuine encouragers, and without them we could never have carried forward the diverse ministries that meant so much to the church. They included those who shared their skills and knowledge in the areas of small business, tailoring, sewing, adult literacy, and children's ministry, and those who addressed refugee issues.

The sewing group, literacy classes, and all other enterprises were a means to help the women and men grow in skill and applying their faith practically in relationships as they worked together. The sewing also made it possible for the women to augment their meager income to meet some of their basic needs for food and shelter. In the initial phase, one agency, *Amani ya Juu* (Higher Peace), provided outlets for women's work. The work is ongoing and a few women have become small entrepreneurs by marketing their wares. Mennonite mission workers Jerry and Ann King-Grosh helped immensely by partnering with us to nurture the spiritual growth of Somalis. They taught Bible studies at retreat, and Ann did a great job of teaching on the biblical view of marriage.

There were five in our family when we went to Kenya. Afrah was five, Sofia was three, and Gedi was six months old. During our early years of ministry, it was common that we had people living with us almost continually. At one time we had thirteen people living in our little home. There were guests for virtually every meal. Many of our guests were refugees, who were coming and going from our home, facing immense challenges and fears. By necessity, we always had a housekeeper. I did my best to help Martha, but much of the burden for hospitality rested upon her. We were both very busy. Martha was teaching part time at Daystar University while carrying much of the load for the hospitality to refugees. She led a Bible study for the Somali women. In addition, she was a wife and mother to three growing and energetic children. I tried to help out as I could.

We were committed to providing food for all who were hungry who came by our home. That was a heavy financial load. Our missionary allowance was not adequate for the needs that pressed around us. Sugar was just one example of our financial challenge. We needed 100 pounds of sugar a month just for those who stopped by for a cup of tea! That did not include the rice needed for those who ate regularly at our table or dropped in casually for a meal. Neither MCC nor EMM wanted to encourage dependency among the refugees from Somalia. These agencies feared that refugees might join the church for food rather than out of genuine faith. So for the first several years of our time in Nairobi our sponsoring agencies resisted providing assistance. However, in 2004 a team from Eastbrook Church visited us. They were a sign that the Lord had not forgotten us and the hungry among whom we served. Thereafter we received regular help from Eastbrook Church for the refugees who needed our assistance. Later EMM and MCC also began to provide hospitality assistance. We were grateful.

Most of our MCC and EMM colleagues did their best to encourage and support us. Some agencies and individuals, however, were indifferent to our work and even opposed it. One visitor had little empathy for our situation and in the presence of Somali refugees accused me of insensitivity toward Martha and the burden she was carrying. Others felt that our church, comprised mostly of refugees, was using funds to induce Muslims to become Christians. I grieved over such accusations.

I was teaching full-time at Daystar University. For awhile I took the bus to the University; but that took at least three hours a day, round trip. Even after we got a car, traffic congestion was terrible and the commute was still two hours. I would get home late afternoon exhausted, yet I would try to meet people who were sipping tea on our lawn, waiting to talk and seeking my advice. I tried to counsel many who came to our home with their challenges and fears. Sometimes they would join us for the evening meal, and conversation would linger into the evening. When they left, I needed to prepare for teaching the next day, as well as grade tests, projects, and papers.

Weekends were filled with church commitments. For a long time the church met at our home on a weekly basis. People would arrive early before the worship service, and often we would serve them a simple lunch afterward of rice, spaghetti, *chapati* (flat bread), and *sukuma wiki* (vegetable greens). The third Saturday of the month we met for an extended time of fellowship and prayer over a meal (Acts 2:42). A few of the worshippers from the fellowship helped prepare the meal, but the coordination of all this fell on Martha.

Our family in mission

Upon our arrival in Nairobi in 1994, Afrah, our oldest, was enrolled at Rosslyn Academy, an international Christian school. As Sofia and Gedi grew old enough, they too enrolled, though they did Kenyan preschool. Rosslyn was a fine school that had been started by EMM in the 1960s and later joined by two other mission agencies. Martha served on the schoolboard for many of the years our children attended the school. We and our children enjoyed the diversity of the student body and the Christian community at Rosslyn, and we appreciated the high academic standards. Our children were very involved in school, but they were also eager helpers when we organized a retreat for the Somali church. Early on, they especially enjoyed working with the children's ministry at the retreats.

Occasionally we took time off as a family. I regret that on several occasions I felt that I could not break away, and so Martha and the children went on vacation without me. Yet we remember with thankfulness the occasions when we as a family, often with the encouragement of our team, had times of reprieve. The policy of our mission was that every three years we were given two months to return to the United States. Every seventh year we were given a year's sabbatical to study, network, renew, and strengthen our relationships. During our home leave times, we visited with our family and friends, shared about our work, strengthened and began new relationships, and sought to learn and grow more in our ability to share Christ's love.

Delight in teaching and peacemaking

I loved teaching, especially because a number of my students came from war-torn countries such as Burundi, Sudan, and Rwanda. Daystar University trusted me to develop a peace studies program, and the courses were very well received. My courses on peacemaking were very relevant to the challenges African students experienced in real life. In chapter five I described some of the peacemaking themes within traditional pre-Islamic Somali culture. Similar themes are found in all traditional African societies. In my courses at Daystar, I developed these themes considerably, to the delight of my students. I also worked with my students as they explored Jesus Christ and the distinctive peace he brings. We explored traditional peacemaking practices as signs that prepared people to receive in fullness the peace offered by Jesus Christ in his life, death, and resurrection. In my courses, I also taught on the significance of the cross in authentic reconciling peacemaking.

During my years in Kenya I continued to be involved in the peace process unfolding in Somalia. For over a year, Somali clan elders met in Nairobi under the leadership of Bethel Kiplegaat, a keen Christian and internationalist. They met in Kenya to be in a safe environment away from the cacophony in Somalia.

For some years clan leaders who were participating in the peace process would come to my home every Wednesday afternoon to consult together on steps forward. We found our traditional culture especially helpful as we explored possibilities, especially the functions of the elders in making and retaining the peace. In modest ways those conversations permeated the peace process unfolding in Nairobi.

Vigorous theological engagement

At another level, Muslim imams would come to our home occasionally for in-depth discussions on matters of faith. Those conversations under the tree in our yard in Nairobi were important in helping to clear up misperceptions about the Christian faith and in exploring the nature of the good news that in Christ we are invited to reconciliation with God and with one another.

This kind of theological encounter for Muslims and Christians usually elicited four basic questions for Muslims. (1) What do you mean when you say "Jesus is the Son of God?" (2) What do you mean by Trinity? (3) How could the Messiah be crucified? (4) Is the Bible corrupted? I could write another book describing our discussions with Muslim theologians and even those who were not theologically trained. Here I will only briefly highlight my approach to these four queries:

1) We do not believe that God has a consort who bore him a son. That is polytheism and a most tragic distortion of the gospel. Rather, "Son of God" is a name that God himself gave to Jesus the Messiah, and so we need to pay attention. What does God mean by that name? The Qur'an opens the door to begin to understand the mystery of who Jesus the Messiah is, for the Qur'an states that he is the Word of God (*Issa Kalimatullah*).[1] Both Muslims and Christians believe that God creates and sustains the universe through his Word. In the Gospel of John we read that in Jesus the Messiah the Word became human and lived among us (John1:14). The Messiah, the Word, came into the world through the Virgin Mary. I think it is significant that Muslims refer to Jesus as the Son of Mary; she is God's chosen servant through whom the one who is the living Word entered the world.

The Word of God cannot be separated from God, for God and his Word are one. Therefore, the Word is the true revelation of God. When we meet Jesus the Messiah, we are meeting the one who is the fullness of the revelation of God. So "Son of God" is one way of expressing that the Messiah is the life-giving living Word of God.

2) God as Trinity does not mean God the Creator, God the mother, and God the Son, as some might think. Muslims believe

that Jesus is both the Spirit of God (*Issa Ruhullah*) and the Word of God (*Issa Kalimatullah*).[2] That understanding can be a step toward understanding the mystery of God as Trinity. Christians believe in God the Creator of all things. God our Creator loves us and seeks us as a shepherd seeking his lost sheep. In Jesus the Messiah, God has entered our history as our Savior, seeking and redeeming sinners from their sinfulness and death. Furthermore, through the Holy Spirit God empowers us to live righteously and to participate in the blessing of loving fellowship with God. God and his Word are one. Likewise, God and his Spirit are one. For that reason when Christians confess God as Father, Son, and Holy Spirit, they are confessing the oneness of God as our loving Savior as well as God present within us through the Holy Spirit.

3) Muslims most often deny the crucifixion of Jesus the Messiah for they believe that Jesus was anointed with the power of God, and the power of God could not suffer defeat. For Christians, however, Jesus was not only crucified, but he also arose from the dead. So they agree that death could not defeat the Messiah; God raised him from the dead! As I have mentioned earlier in this book, there are signs within Islam and traditional African religion pointing to the crucifixion of Jesus. These signs include the lambs that are sacrificed and the Qur'anic description of the "tremendous" substitutionary sacrifice of a ram to save a son of Abraham from death.[3] These sacrifices point to Jesus, the Lamb of God who takes away the sin of the world! As Jesus died with his outstretched arms on the cross, he cried out in forgiveness. His open arms on the cross are God's invitation to us to receive forgiveness and to be reconciled to God.

4) Muslims believe that God is almighty and would never permit his revelation to be corrupted. For this reason both the Qur'an and Muhammad have a very high respect for the Bible and do not teach that the Bible is corrupted. In fact, in regard to scriptures and prophets before the coming of Muhammad, the Qur'an proclaims that no one can alter the Word of God. This surely refers to the Bible.[4]

There are thousands of ancient biblical manuscripts from before the time of Muhammad which show that the Hebrew

Old Testament and Greek New Testament we have today are trustworthy transmissions of the original texts. We can say with confidence that God and the people of God have faithfully preserved his Word. The Bible reveals God and his message to humankind; it is through the Bible that we meet Jesus who is the living Word of God in human form.

These are my responses to four key questions that Muslims often present to Christians. My responses illustrate the way I responded to these kinds of questions as I met with Muslim leaders and theologians in Nairobi and elsewhere. If possible, I would begin with the Muslim scriptures but then introduce them to biblical revelation and the Christ whom the Bible reveals. In the book of Acts, we discover Paul using a similar approach when he met Greek philosophers on Mars Hill; he first quoted from their poets (Acts 17:22-34). It was also the approach we had used thirty years earlier when developing the *People of God* Bible study for Muslims. This approach is like a bridge to those who are considering the gospel.

These Nairobi gatherings with a small cluster of Muslim scholars were significant in building trust. Of course, hospitality was key, and Martha was involved in hosting, meal preparation, and making people feel welcome. The scholars appreciated my responses to their questions. Consequently they became my advocates as well as advocates for Somali believers in Christ within the Islamic community. On at least one occasion we invited others to participate in these discussions, such as Harold Miller, a respected Christian peace advocate. These remarkable conversations continued until we needed to leave Kenya.

Joyous fruitfulness

Our years in Nairobi were very good! We were perched on the edges, as it were, of the high drama unfolding in Somalia. Yet from that position we were able to engage in the call of God to serve as ambassadors of the gospel of reconciliation. The special challenges were for us as Church to really be a community of reconciliation. The Church is the only community on earth that believes that a crucified and risen Savior is central to God's grand design to bring all things in heaven and earth into reconciliation with God. Yet that grand plan needs to be revealed within the church.

In our sojourn in Nairobi, the Somali church was often a fractured community—yet we were nevertheless a people redeemed by the grace of God in Jesus Christ and bearing witness to the reconciliation that is ours in Christ. The joyous songs of the children at our weekly worship bore witness to the joy of reconciliation.

We experienced other signs of reconciliation as well. In 1999 many Somali believers met at a retreat center outside Addis Ababa, Ethiopia. They came from at least a dozen countries, representing Somalis both inside and outside the country. It was a marvelous time for cultivating reconciled relationships.

In July 2004 another gathering of Somali believers in Christ convened outside Nairobi. Somalis came from the whole eastern Africa region. At least one person participated from each Somali clan. Something happened that we had never witnessed before. Persons representing each clan confessed their sins of hostility toward the other clans and then prayed for forgiveness and reconciliation. On behalf of the Somali nation, the assembly also requested forgiveness from Eastern Mennonite Missions for the 1962 killing of Merlin Grove, one of the early EMM mission directors in Somalia. Heaven touched earth as we shared in that marvelous gathering.

CHAPTER 10

Christ Is My Center
Reflection on My Destiny
(2009–2010)

*I press on toward the goal to win the prize for which
God has called me heavenward in Christ Jesus.*
—Apostle Paul

W E are grateful for the fifteen years we served in Nairobi and
for the expanding fruitfulness of our ministries among the
Somali people. But near the end of that time, in 2006, came a
big surprise: I was diagnosed with prostate cancer. Initially I
responded well to the treatment. I remembered that God had
intervened in my life dramatically in the past to rescue me from
death. Surely he would intervene again now. Yet the disease progressed. Finally I could not continue with my responsibilities in
Nairobi. We needed to return to the United States for more
medical care. So, in 2009 our family prepared to return. Upon
our arrival in Chicago, Mari and Don Chevako met us and
drove us to Milwaukee. We were welcomed back home and
have been blessed and encouraged by friends, family, and our
community of faith.

A time for reflection

The discovery of cancer began a time of soul searching. I was
told that suppressed anger can contribute to prostate cancer. I
have always resisted nurturing resentment in my soul. My
approach to life has always been to confront anything that gives

me anger. I confront, and then let go, and I do not revisit the situation. If a person is functioning in ways that I believe are destructive to the church or others, I will confront, sometimes very forthrightly. But I do not keep revisiting the wrong that has been done or the person I have disagreed with. After the confrontation, I leave the matter between that person and the Lord, and I press on with my responsibilities.

Yet even so, perhaps there is suppressed anger within me. For example, I become agitated whenever I think of those immodest baptisms I commented on in chapter nine. That really angers me. I am also angry that the missionaries closed the church shortly after our arrival in Nairobi. I confronted my feelings then, but perhaps I have not let go as I should have. So I am asking the Holy Spirit to search my heart so that I may be truly free of all anger and bitterness. I want to live every day as a forgiven and forgiving man.

I have always been a dynamo of activism. I have a passion for the church and a vision to see the Somali church thrive as an indigenous movement bearing witness to the gospel among all Somali clans. Consequently I have never invested much time sitting at the feet of Jesus, as Mary did and whom Jesus commended for her listening quietude (Luke 10:39-42). I don't have time for that. I serve Jesus; the times of quiet alone with Jesus are rather rare for me. I should learn from Mary.

However, my activism does not mean that I do not have a relationship with Jesus. He is, in fact, my very best friend, and from the moment I arise in the morning until I retire at night I am in active prayer with Jesus. In my experience Jesus is much like Mark's Gospel describes him, taking his disciples "immediately" from one engagement to another. Although I am an activist, I am never alone, for Jesus is always with me. So my times with the Lord are all day long!

The Word of God is important for me. Martha and I try to have a time reading the Word together daily with the children. During the summer of our arrival in the United States in 2009, we were separated as a family due to my cancer treatments. During this time we told our two youngest children which Bible passages we were reading. This was to encourage them to read the same passage. So even though we were separated for a time, we were still united in reading the same biblical portions.

The church has been a community of caring support during all the challenges we have experienced, including the current cancer health crisis. The church is the only community on earth that believes that God is fully revealed in Jesus, that in the cross we are reconciled to God and to one another. It is in the church that this radical life-giving faith is nurtured. Without the church I would never have survived as a Christian. My spiritual formation and commitments have been shaped within me as I participate in the fellowship of believers Sunday after Sunday. It is in the meeting of believers that I meet Jesus week by week standing in our midst.

Marc and Nancy Erickson have been wonderful hosts for Martha and me as I have undergone one medical procedure after another. Some of the procedures have been very difficult. Yet there have been times of reprieve as well. This has provided opportunities to invest precious hours with our family. A highlight was attending a basketball game in which my son Gedi played. In Nairobi I used to cheer so loudly at my children's sports events that my sons tell me my voice overwhelmed all the other shouting and cheering at those games. Now, however, my illness mutes my shouting, but my heart cheers mightily.

Death and hope

For some time we resisted talking about the possibility of death. In Africa I knew that on several occasions the Lord had raised me up from the threshold of death. Now, back in the United States, I believed God would do so again. One reason for this conviction was that there was so much more I wanted to accomplish in Somali ministries in East Africa. Our fifteen years in Nairobi had only laid some foundations for ongoing ministries. We longed to return to bring greater completion to what we had begun. One core dimension of that commitment was peacemaking in Somalia. I longed to continue the peacemaking forums with elders and imams who had convened under the tree in our yard in Nairobi. I assumed that that was our future.

Yet, in time we began to talk about the possibility of my death. Those have been important conversations for me and my family. As our family has opened up to talk about death, I was also able to talk with friends about it. That has been freeing. Indeed, for me to live or die is Christ; either way I shall continue to serve him with joy, whether in this life, or in his coming kingdom. Yet, as Paul did in writing to the Philippians, I hope to live, for there is still so much ministry that I envisage.

A farewell journey to Kenya

A special joy for us was returning to Kenya in April 2010, a year after our move back to the United States. Although I was very ill, the Lord revived me for that trip. Two of our children accompanied us. Unless the Lord would touch me dramatically with healing, this would be our farewell journey. Somali clan elders met with me. We met with a variety of friends from the University. We had a wonderful time reconnecting with the Somali community, and for Martha it was a joy to meet with the women's sewing group that she had invested in so energetically.

A highlight was our meeting with the Somali church and my special time with its elders. I urged the church to maintain the unity of the Spirit and to press on to know Jesus Christ. I preached on the cross and resurrection of Jesus Christ and its centrality to our salvation and to our reconciliation with God and one another. I reminded them that in our traditional Somali culture, when a baby or even an adult was ill, we would sacrifice a lamb. We would take the blood of the lamb and bathe the ill person in that blood for healing. We know that blood heals. I then reminded them that Jesus is the Lamb of God who has shed his blood for our forgiveness and healing. We are healed, cleansed, and forgiven through the blood of Jesus. That was my farewell sermon! We parted knowing that our farewell was not final, for we will most certainly meet again in eternity in that joyous reunion with our Lord Jesus Christ.

Writing my story

One of the blessings of my illness has been working with David and Grace Shenk in developing these memoirs. Several months after our return to the United States we met at the home of our mutual friends Kenneth and Elizabeth Nissley. I told the Shenks that I wanted David to write my story. We have known each other for many years, and they had lived among the Somali people. Although David and Grace are abroad many months each year, they committed to doing what they could to write these memoirs. It has been a special blessing to meet with them for many hours as they listened to my story.

I wanted my memoirs to be written for several reasons. First, I have a story to tell that I want both Muslims and Christians to know. Second, I want people to know that Jesus Christ called me to be his ambassador. Third, I want to make it clear that my Muslim heritage prepared me to hear and believe the gospel. Fourth, I want my children and future grandchildren to know my story, for I long for them to cherish the Christ who is the center of my life. I want those four themes to be woven into my story as it is written and shared extensively. My story is really God's story, for it is God who has called me and commissioned me to be an ambassador of the gospel of peace within the world of Islam and especially among the Somali people.

Paul writes that we all see through a glass darkly. This is my story as I see it. My assessment of the path I have taken might not be the way others see it. I ask the forgiveness of those who will feel that I have not accurately presented their part of the story, for my story intersects with hundreds of others. This calls for grace. My prayer is that my story as I have shared it will bring glory to the Lord Jesus Christ who is my Center Pole and will be an encouragement to the church that is my home.

EPILOGUE

Our Journey
Martha Jean Wilson Haile

THE journey that God has led us on has been truly something that only God could do. As I reflect on the twenty-three years of our ministry and life together, the challenges, obstacles, and surprises we have met on the way, the hand of God has been always present. Ahmed has always held a deep and abiding love for his country and for his people. Even as our friendship was growing, Ahmed explicitly stated to me his commitment to his family, his people, and his country.

My faith journey has been very different than Ahmed's, and in many ways I have traveled a steep learning curve. I entered the body of Christ through the door of salvation at the Second Missionary Baptist Church in Richmond, Indiana, as a young child at a summer vacation Bible school. It was there my foundations were established and my journey began. From that beginning I have learned much from many in the body of Christ, the church, and from the Shepherd who leads us.

In numerous ways we have been blessed, strengthened, and enriched by friends, family, and the body of Christ. The diversity and unity of the body of Christ also challenges me. I have learned much on this journey, and I am still learning.

Throughout my time in Mogadishu, preparing and serving tea to many was the backdrop of our daily life. Tea-drinking hospitality was woven into the fabric of the culture. Throughout our time in Nairobi, it was the same. Drinking tea together symbolized our willingness and desire to get to know others. Hospitality was and still is important in our home. Not to be confused with entertaining, hospitality meant welcoming people into our hearts and home. As our children noted, this was not always convenient. Undergirding all of what we did was the mat of hospitality and the attitude of openness and welcome.

The diversity in the world and among people is astounding. The love of God and the plan of God for this creation are awe-inspiring. God desires to have a living loving relationship with everyone.

My prayer is that Ahmed's story will help us all grow in understanding and appreciation for one another's faith journeys, educating us to the fact that in every culture God has already left markers for the ultimate journey and draws many more into the hut where Jesus is the Center Pole.

May God richly bless you,
Allah ha'idiin barakeeyo

Questions for Reflection and Discussion

David W. Shenk

THESE questions are organized in twelve segments, one for each of the ten chapters in the book, as well as a segment for the introductory section and a final segment for considering the implications of Ahmed's journey for each of us personally. The book is well suited for study groups who wish to use this book for a thirteen-week, three-month study. For a thirteenth segment, study groups might invite a resource person who knows the Muslim world well to share from their experience.

Ahmed's journey has been significantly formed by the Scriptures, which is reflected in the inclusion of a suggested background scripture for each chapter. In the mosque where Ahmed grew up, whenever there was any matter to be discussed, the imam always read a relevant portion of the Qur'an first. Likewise, we suggest that the background scripture be read meditatively at the beginning of each discussion time.

Foreword/Preface
Scripture: Acts 22:1-22

1. Dudley Woodberry writes in his foreword that Ahmed's journey has much to offer in our world plagued with inter-religious and inter-ethnic strife. Identify and discuss the resources for peacemaking that Dudley highlights.

2. Why did Ahmed believe that his story should be written? What did he hope Muslims would learn? What would be the contribution for Christians?

3. What is the significance of the children's response to the question of what should be included in their father's story?

4. What is the significance of hospitality in your life and in the life of your community or church?

Chapter 1: Muslim-Somali Heritage
Scripture: Jeremiah 35:1-11

1. What values of Ahmed's family were most significant in forming his leadership qualities? What wisdom and character traits did Ahmed acquire from his father?

2. Describe the values that Ahmed absorbed through Somali proverbs and narratives.

3. Ahmed often says, "I will never speak critically of Islam." What did he experience within his Muslim heritage that he considered especially valuable?

4. Which do you think was the most formative for him, Islam or his traditional Somali heritage? Give reasons for your response to that question.

5. What were the questions and yearnings of his boyhood soul that opened his heart to an interest in the gospel?

Chapter 2: From Islam to the Gospel
Scripture: 1 Peter 1:18-20; 1 Peter 2:9-10

1. Reflect on Ahmed's journey from Islam to the gospel. In what ways do you discern the ministry of the Holy Spirit upon Ahmed in that journey?

2. Reflect on Ahmed's conversion. What was the role of Christians in leading Ahmed to faith in Jesus Christ? What can we learn from Ahmed's account about our own reaching out to those who have not yet believed in Christ?

3. Ahmed says that when he committed to Jesus Christ and the church, he had come home. In what ways had he come home?

4. He asserts that the mosque is not the church. What are the similarities? What are the differences?

5. Many Muslims who believe in Christ continue to worship in the mosque at least for some time. Ahmed states clearly that he never did that. What are the reasons for his decision to make such a clean break? How do you respond to that choice?

6. Comment on ways that a Somali nomadic home is a metaphor for the church. In what ways is that metaphor helpful in understanding the nature of the church?

Chapter 3: Christ or Success
Scripture: Luke 9:57-62

1. In 1964, when Ahmed was eleven, the SIM closed their school in Bulo Burte rather than permit Islam to be taught in their school. SMM decided to permit Islam to be taught rather than close their schools. What counsel would you have given to SIM and SMM in regard to this requirement?

2. Why did Ahmed choose Jesus Christ rather than success?

3. Imagine the farewell at his home in Bulo Burte as he was preparing to leave for Kenya. How did his father respond? What did that response mean for Ahmed?

4. Describe ways that Ahmed experienced the Lord as his Good Shepherd on his journey into the future as he left Somalia. Identify times in your life when you experienced the Lord as the Good Shepherd.

5. Ahmed often refers to the Word of Life Camp and the Bible study on Philippians (2:1-11; 3:4-8) as a worldview transformation. What is it about those passages that so clearly defined for Ahmed the difference between Islam and the gospel?

6. Describe the differences between Ahmed's life in Nairobi and his boyhood in Bulo Burte. How did he maintain faith and character within the tempting voices of Nairobi urban life?

Chapter 4: Pursuing Education
Scripture: Philippians 4:8-19

1. What was the role of the church and friends in facilitating Ahmed's studies? In what ways did WMHS help Ahmed make his transition into North America? What can we learn from his experience about encouraging emerging leaders?

2. How did his mother's advice about one-eyed people help Ahmed cope with cultural diversity? How do you assess her advice?

3. Imagine a person from a very conservative village in Somalia plunging into studies at a North American college or university. Reflect on the differences. How did Ahmed maintain his center and positive spirit within such enormously different contexts?

4. What was the role of Christian friends in encouraging

Ahmed? What can be learned from Ahmed's experience about hospitality for international students?

5. Reflect on Ahmed's decision to pursue peace studies. What were key influences leading him to make that choice?

6. During his final months at Goshen College, events transpired in far off regions of the Muslim world that would impact Ahmed's life and ministry significantly. What were those events and in what ways would these events in the course of time affect Christian-Muslim relations?

Chapter 5: Serving Within Muslim Society
Scripture: Acts 15:1-11

1. In what ways did the Somali proverb that a man who does not see the world is blind help Ahmed relate to the enormous transitions he had experienced during his eight years abroad? In what ways did the same principles equip him for the transition back to his home community?

2. The Nigerian writer, Chinua Achebe, writes that things fall apart when there is no center. Ahmed writes about his center that gives him confidence and focus. Describe Ahmed's center.

3. What is your response to Ahmed's theory of social and cultural change? What do you think of his observations of the role of the church in social change?

4. What are the pluses and minuses of a community development leader such as Ahmed being involved in the church within a Muslim society? How do you respond to Ahmed's decision to clearly identify with the church?

5. Assess Ahmed's approach to conflict transformation and peacemaking.

6. Imagine Ahmed's role as director of Eastbrook Development Program in Somalia. What were the special challenges he faced directing a foreign-based agency while maintaining his credibility with his home community?

Chapter 6: Struggle for Inclusion
Scripture: Acts 21:26–22:2

1. What were the reasons for the determination by some leaders of Ahmed's clan that he must die?

2. How did Ahmed earn the right to be included within Muslim Somali society? What was Martha's role in that process?

3. How do you account for the transformation in the soul of the imam who at one time led the death threats and opposition to Ahmed, and later blessed Ahmed and his ministry, and who at considerable risk to his life led the Eastbrook team to safety?

4. How do you respond to Ahmed's persistent participation in the church in the face of enormous pressures to desist?

5. Ahmed likens the Muslim minaret with its call to prayer to the call of Jesus Christ for his disciples to be his witnesses. Describe some of the ways that Ahmed shared his witness for Christ.

Chapter 7: Wounded Peacemaker
Scripture: Matthew 5:1-16

1. Describe the peacemaking mission of Ergo. Assess the validity and effectiveness of this kind of interfaith effort in peacemaking.

2. Describe the different peacemaking themes that are present in traditional Somali society, Islam, and the gospel. What is the difference between peacemaking and the gift of reconciliation that Christ offers? What do you think of the way Ahmed works with these different themes in his peacemaking effort?

3. How do you respond to Ahmed's description of the distinctive contribution of Jesus Christ in peacemaking? In what ways are the traditional animal sacrifices signs pointing to the reconciling sacrifice of Christ? What is René Girard's contribution to that question?

4. Why did Aidid and his cohorts determine that Ahmed must be killed?

5. Review the many ways God's providential care for Ahmed was revealed after the rocket attack.

Chapter 8: Foundation for Peacemaking
Scripture: Ephesians 2:14-19; Romans 12:9-21

1. Describe the nature of the peace of Islam.

2. Consider ways that the Muslim community as described in this narrative worked at peacemaking.

3. Describe the peace of Christ.

4. Consider ways that the church as described in this narrative expressed the peace of Christ.

5. In what ways did Ahmed serve as an ambassador of the gospel of reconciliation? What has surprised you about his approach? How do you assess his mission as an ambassador of the peace of Christ?

6. Ahmed highlights a variety of scriptures as he explores the essence of Christ-centered peace and reconciliation: Philippians 2:1-11; Ephesians 2:14; 2 Corinthians 5:18-21; Romans 12:14-21. Select one or several of these scriptures and reflect on the ways that the gospel of reconciliation as described in the passage(s) was expressed through the ministries of Ahmed and Martha.

Chapter 9: Hope Within Conflict
Scripture: Philippians 2:1-11

1. What were some positive as well as negative ways that mission and service agencies affected the well-being of the Somali church? What principles should guide mission and service agencies in relating to emerging churches within Muslim contexts?

2. Describe the role of intercessory prayer in the healing and rebirth of the church. Share other examples from your experience of the church in prayer finding the way through seemingly hopeless obstacles.

3. Describe the enormous challenges to family life experienced by Ahmed and Martha and their children. How did the family respond to those challenges?

4. Ahmed explored peacemaking approaches with the clan elders as they met week by week under his tree in Nairobi. As you think about their Somali and Muslim values, what ideas for peacemaking do you think they talked about as persons who were respected as leaders? What surprises derived from the gospel do you think Ahmed might have contributed within those discussions?

5. What is your assessment of Ahmed's response to the four questions Muslims bring to the table when they converse with

Christians about faith and theology? What was the role of Martha and the children in facilitating these conversations?

Chapter 10: Christ Is My Center
Scripture: Philippians 1:18-27

1. What are the surprises in Ahmed's spiritual formation?

2. How does Ahmed view the possibility of death at a time when his apostolic calling is flourishing?

3. What is especially poignant in Ahmed's reflections on his journey with Jesus Christ as he struggles with the ravages of cancer?

4. What were the significant highlights of his final message of encouragement to the elders of the Somali church in Kenya?

Concluding Reflection
Scripture: 1 John 1:1-4

1. In what ways have your understandings of Islam and Muslims changed as you have followed Ahmed's journey? What has surprised you?

2. As you finish reading Ahmed's journey, revisit again his assertion that Islam was a preparation for him to believe the gospel. What does he mean by that statement? It is also possible that for some Muslims their understanding of Islam influences them to turn away from the gospel. Comment on examples of that happening in Ahmed's narrative.

3. Ahmed believed that he was called of God to be an ambassador of Christ, an emissary of the peace of the gospel within the world of Islam and especially among the Somali people. How do you evaluate the fruitfulness of Ahmed's calling? What is the nature of fruitfulness within the kingdom of God?

4. In what ways has Ahmed's journey deepened your appreciation for the gospel of Jesus Christ and the reconciliation he offers?

5. What has been especially significant for you as you have followed Ahmed's journey?

Endnotes

Chapter 1: Muslim-Somali Heritage

1. Social capital refers to the true wealth of a society: the values that contribute to enhancing social well-being. For example, a society might have abundant material resources such as diamonds in the river beds, yet be awash with violence. That is a society with a serious deficit of social capital. It is important that societies cherish and develop social capital. In Bulo Burte when I was a boy, one way our social capital developed was through the introduction of modern education, even for girls. We had little money, but we were a healthy society in the sense that we were a civil people. For a helpful elaboration on the role of social capital in community and personal well-being, I recommend James S. Coleman, *Foundations of Social Theory* (Boston: Harvard University Press, 1990), 300–321.

2. Qur'an, *Al-Ikhlas* (the Purity of Faith): surah 112.

3. Messiah is the Semitic word for Christ, which is derived from the Greek. In these memoirs we use Christ and Messiah interchangeably. Although Muslims believe Jesus is the Messiah, the Qur'an does not develop the meaning of Jesus as the Messiah.

Chapter 3: Christ or Success

1. Some time later in the United States I met the daughter of one of these men at a time when she was in distress. I helped her generously, choosing not to return upon her what I had experienced from her father.

2. Tarif Khalidi, *The Muslim Jesus* (Cambridge, MA: Harvard University Press, 2001), 15.

Chapter 5: Serving Within Muslim Society

1. Chinua Achebe, *Things Fall Apart* (New York: Anchor Books, 1959).

2. John Paul Lederach has been quite engaged as a consultant for the Somali peace process. He has written extensively, but a particularly pertinent book is his *Little Book of Conflict Transformation* (Intercourse, PA: Good Books, 2003).

3. William Butler Yeats, *Michael Robartes and the Dancer* (Churchtown, Dundrum, Ireland: The Chuala Press, 1920).

Chapter 6: Struggle for Inclusion

1. Qur'an, *Nisaa* (The Women): surah 4:171. Although the Qur'an refers to Jesus as *Kalimatullah*, most Muslim theologians assert that this does not mean incarnation, but rather that God spoke and Jesus was created in the womb of the virgin. Yet Christians perceive that this statement in regard to Jesus might open the door for the consideration of incarnation.

Chapter 7: Wounded Peacemaker

1. René Girard, *Violence and the Sacred,* trans. Patrick Gregory (Baltimore: John Hopkins University Press, 1972), 1-76, 250–273.

Chapter 8: Foundation for Peacemaking

1. Robert G. Clouse, *War: Four Christian Views* (Downers Grove, IL: Intervarsity Press, 1981).

Chapter 9: Hope Within Conflict

1. Qur'an, *Nisaa* (The Women): surah 4:171.
2. Qur'an, *Nisaa* (The Women): surah 4:171.
3. Qur'an, *Saffat* (Those Ranged in Ranks): surah 37:107.
4. Qur'an, *Anam* (The Cattle): surah 6:34.

About the Author and Editor

AHMED Ali Haile was born in Bulo Burte, Somalia, into a loving Muslim family where hospitality and respect were valued. He became a devout young student of the Qu'ran. Then, at a tumultuous time in his country's history, he discovered Jesus Christ and the transforming power of his love. In response to his growing convictions about the centrality of Christ in the peace of God, he turned down the opportunity for political advancement in his country and left for Kenya and later to the United States.

In the United States, Ahmed pursued degrees related to community development with special focus in peace and conflict transformation. In 1982, desiring to help his homeland, he traveled back to Somalia to work in development and peace among his people. He married Martha J. Wilson in 1987 and they established a home in Somalia. Even as the country descended into chaos and they had to leave the country, Ahmed nurtured his call to bring warring Somali groups together. In 1992, when on one of several peacemaking missions to Mogadishu, a rocket-propelled grenade shattered his leg.

For fifteen years Ahmed taught peace studies at Daystar University in Nairobi, Kenya, where many of his students were from war-torn countries, including Somalia. The family returned to the United States in 2009 and settled in Glendale, Wisconsin. Ahmed and Martha have three children—Afrah, Sofia, and Gedi.

DAVID W. Shenk has lived much of his life in East Africa, where his parents were pioneer missionaries with Eastern Mennonite Missions. He and his wife, Grace, worked sixteen years in Soma-

lia and Kenya with a special focus on education within Muslim
contexts. A pastor, church planter, and teacher, he has also served
in international global church networking and missions, most
recently as academic dean at the Lithuania Christian College. At
present he is Global Consultant with Eastern Mennonite Missions.

His interest in relevant Christian presence, peacemaking, and
witness in a world of religious pluralism—especially among
Muslims—has taken him into more than 100 countries. He has
usually traveled as a presenter in seminars or in dialogical
engagements with Muslims, including a formal dialogue with
theologians in Qom, Iran. He has authored or edited seventeen
books or booklets and written numerous articles on themes
related to the gospel and peacemaking in a pluralist world. *A
Muslim and Christian in Dialogue* and *Journeys of the Muslim
Nation and the Christian Church*, in particular, are companions
to *Teatime in Mogadishu*.

David has taught in a variety of universities and seminaries in
the United States and internationally. He holds a doctorate in
religious studies education from New York University, with
course work in anthropology. He and Grace have four children
and seven grandchildren. They live in Mountville, Pennsylvania.